D0471543

Contemporary Crafts

Decorative Paper Crafts

VIVIEN FRANK

Contemporary Crafts

Decorative Paper Crafts

Vivien Frank

**TIGER BOOKS
INTERNATIONAL**

First published in 1991 by Letts of London
an imprint of New Holland Publishers (UK) Ltd
London • Cape Town • Sydney • Singapore

24 Nutford Place
London W1H 6DQ
United Kingdom

80 McKenzie Street
Cape Town 8001
South Africa

3/2 Aquatic Drive
Frenchs Forest, NSW 2086
Australia

This edition published in 1998 by
Tiger Books International Plc, Twickenham, U.K.

ISBN 1 84056 018 5

Copyright © 1991 Charles Letts & Co Ltd

All rights reserved. No part of this publication may be
reproduced, stored in a retrieval system, or transmitted
in any form or by any means, electronic, mechanical,
photocopying, recording or otherwise, without the prior
written permission of the publishers and copyright holders.

Printed and bound in Singapore by Tien Wah Press (Pte) Ltd

2 4 6 8 10 9 7 5 3 1

Publisher's Note
The author and publisher have made every effort to ensure that all
instructions contained within this book are accurate and safe, and therefore
they cannot accept liability for any resulting injury, damage or loss to
persons or property however it may arise.

Acknowledgments
The author and publisher would like to thank the following people for
kindly loaning material to be photographed for the Gallery section of this
book: Sarah Amatt, Lisa von Clemm, Compton Marbling, Dalma
Flanders, Frances Greenburgh, Dennis Hall at John Perry, Martin
Lawrence; Paul Jackson and Florence Tenko for permission to use designs.
The author is most grateful for the creative assistance of Caroline Frank
and Diana Thomson. The pictures by Susan Kinley and Gregory Warren
Wilson were commissioned by the author especially for the book.

CONTENTS

INTRODUCTION   *6*

GALLERY   *8*

DECORATING TECHNIQUES   *16*

MATERIALS AND EQUIPMENT   *28*

BASIC TECHNIQUES   *30*

GLOSSARY   *35*

PROJECTS

WRITING PAPER AND GREETINGS CARDS   *37*

NOTELET CASE   *43*

GIFT BAGS   *47*

BOX COVER   *51*

WASTEPAPER CONTAINER   *55*

LAMPSHADES   *59*

PICTURE MOUNT   *67*

PICTURE FRAME   *71*

BLOTTER AND LETTER HOLDER   *77*

LETTER PORTFOLIO   *83*

PHOTOGRAPH ALBUM COVER AND
PHOTOGRAPH ALBUM   *91*

SUPPLIERS AND INDEX   *96*

INTRODUCTION

ONE OF MY main aims in writing this book has been to communicate to the reader the versatility of both the material – paper – and the techniques of decoration. Paper is a wonderful invention, which people usually take for granted. This attitude is probably the result of familiarity – paper is so much a part of everyday life that one does not stop to consider either how it is made, what it is made from, or the many ways in which it is used.

Paper can be defined as a substance made from cellulose fibres extracted from rags, wood or straw and formed into thin, flat sheets. Sometimes other additives are included in the paper pulp, depending on its final use and the manner of its making. Most of the paper in general use today is machine-made. The paper is formed when the pulp comes into contact with a rotating mesh cylinder and is then passed over a series of rollers along a moving belt – draining and drying the length of paper prior to cutting it into sheets. Handmade paper is formed on a 'mould', drained on a bed of felt and left to dry in a pile with other sheets. It is for this reason that it is important to know how the paper has been made – handmade paper does not have a 'grain' direction, as the fibres are evenly shaken on the 'mould'; in machine-made papers the fibres settle in the direction of the moving belt. With a little basic knowledge and some experience, one can soon develop an appreciation of the various qualities of paper and an understanding of the paper's reaction to different treatments. For example, a sheet of handmade paper has a completely different 'feel' to a sheet of machine-made paper with a very smooth 'hot press' finish – two such dissimilar papers could not be used for the same project. There are books available with detailed information on papermaking materials and techniques.

Paper is used, and abused, in an immense variety of ways – from the mundane to the exotic. Paper is used to satisfy our daily needs at every level: anything from money to packaging, communication to clothes. Paper is also used in many decorative and artistic forms from wallpaper and paintings to papier mâché articles and home accessories. Paper used in these ways is often decorated with patterns and it is the creation of such decorative effects with which this book mainly concerns itself and sets out to explain.

Immediately following this introduction the reader can enjoy beautiful photographs showing the very diverse works of a dozen or so different artists and craftspersons.

Paper can be decorated in an enormous number of ways of which only a few can be explained in the following pages. However, if the reader enjoys the techniques shown here, alternative methods can be explored and discovered either from other books or simply by experimentation – the whole process of decorating and working with paper quickly becomes addictive and highly satisfying.

Paper has been decorated almost since its invention and there is evidence of marbled papers as early as the 12th century. There are also indications that some papers were decorated to foil copyists and forgers – important documents were written on highly decorated paper and – to deter thieves – the edges of books were marbled so that any missing pages would be noticed at once. It is likely that most decorated papers were originally intended for the bookbinding trade and there are many early examples of endpapers and book wrappers. Patterns for printed textiles are usually designed first on paper and often these are then used as decorated papers in their own right, as well as being converted into

printed or woven fabrics.

Preceding the projects section of the book, there is an important section on the composition of paper and the basic techniques, which will recur throughout that section. The reader should resist all temptation to skim over these pages as they contain a wealth of information and explain methods that must be used throughout the rest of the book.

The section of the book concerned with the making of objects can, of course, be used without having first decorated your own papers. However, I hope that the added satisfaction of applying your own design and embellishment to the paper, and thus controlling the project from beginning to end, will spur you to use both sections of the book. Another less esoteric incentive to make your own papers is that you can produce wonderful articles for a comparatively small financial outlay; all the components and materials used are, for the main part, readily available. The projects range from the most simple to the relatively complex but few require specialized equipment. The projects show uncomplicated ideas and should encourage you to develop new skills: they have been arranged in order progressing from the basic printing of writing paper, through the making and presentation of gifts, to the designing and creation of photograph albums. Each project uses a decorated paper but the different papers are often interchangeable. The suitability of the paper is discussed at the beginning of each project.

When decorating papers, it is important that you feel free to experiment both with the technique and the design. It really is not necessary to be artistic in order to create decorated papers and transform them into something more permanent. It is only necessary to be creative, to wish to attempt new procedures and to develop fresh skills.

. . . .

The selection of papers on the right shows the decorative effects, from top to bottom, of marbling (with size), paste, lino-cut block printing, and folding and dyeing. The background to these pages was also marbled using a simpler method without size.

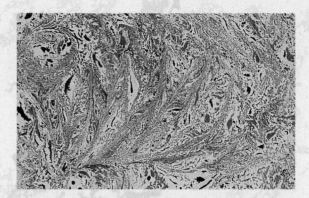

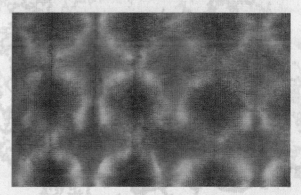

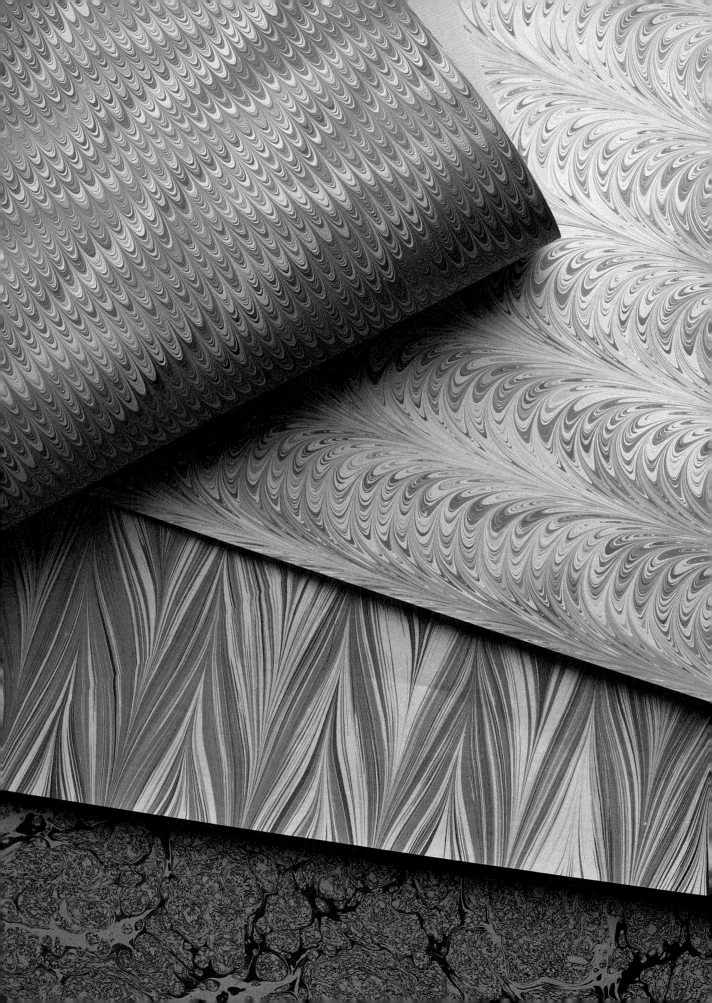

GALLERY

THIS SECTION aims to whet the reader's appetite and to give an idea of the versatility of paper and the variety of decorative effects that can be achieved. These pieces are intended to stimulate the imagination and to show the way in which people, other than the author, embellish and employ paper. The manner of creating these compositions is not described, although some of the contributors have kindly supplied statements about how and why they work in the way they do.

~

SARAH AMATT began her career as a hand bookbinder with paper marbling as a side interest, which gradually became more important to her. She read all the old manuals she could find in museums and then set about teaching herself by trial and error. Sarah experimented with both oil-based and water-based inks and has now marbled full-time for three years. She produces both traditional and non-traditional combed and 'stone' patterns. Her papers have been reproduced for book jackets and stationery and even for stamp borders by the Post Office. The designs shown here are traditional combed patterns in contemporary colours.

. . . .

JOHN PERRY – *Block printed wallpapers.*
The wallpapers produced at the John Perry factory are still printed using traditional block printing methods. This company has an international business and specializes in high quality production. Many of the orders taken are 'one off' commissions for specific properties. English Heritage and the National Trust are some of the clients who request wallpapers to be printed to refurbish some of the houses under their supervision. John Perry has over 3,000 hand-cut wood blocks stored in the cellars and, despite being up to 200 years old, some of these blocks are still in use to this day. The company was responsible for the wallpapers made for the recent Washington D.C. exhibition, 'Treasure Houses of Britain'.

. . . .

Top left. 'Gothic Lily' – This is one of many wallpapers designed by Pugin, who was a 19th-century British architect, who helped restore the Palace of Westminster, between 1840 and 1850. This particular design was for the House of Commons. It is not shown in its original colours. It remains an extremely popular design and is used for grand, gothic-style places.

. . . .

Middle left. 'Strawberry' designed by Pugin for the House of Lords – whose heraldic emblem is the strawberry – during the restoration of the Palace of Westminster. Again, the design is not shown in its original colours.

. . . .

Bottom left. 'Crace Diaper', another Pugin design; although it is named after Crace who cut the blocks and printed the papers. This was a domestic pattern used in the apartments at the Palace of Westminster and is shown here in an authentic and traditional colour.

. . . .

Top right. This paper was designed in the late 19th century by Owen Jones, a Victorian designer and architectural historian. He was responsible for designing the Great Exhibition. This pattern comes from his seminal work *The Grammar of Ornament*. It is a well balanced small design and is widely used to this day. It can be printed in several different colours.

. . . .

Middle right. This design has a strong Persian influence but has no known history. The design is very reminiscent of motifs at the Alhambra in Spain. It probably dates from the mid 19th century. The block was found in the John Perry collection and may have been one of the blocks acquired by John Perry from a smaller company.

. . . .

Bottom right. This is another design, c.1840– 1850, created by Pugin during the Palace of Westminster restoration, this time for the House of Commons Tea Room. It features coronets, portcullises and Tudor roses.

. . . .

These beautiful pieces were found in Kenya, where they were obviously created using local flowers, which have been lightly pressed. The paper is probably made from paper pulp and the flowers have been carefully arranged to look like a bouquet. A thin layer of paper pulp has then been placed over the flowers to affix them to the base sheet. In most paper-making incorporating flowers, the positioning of the flowers is more random and they would be embedded deeper in the pulp. *Above.*

. . . .

FRANCES GREENBURGH is a basketmaker and works mainly with cane. She sometimes incorporates other materials into her basketmaking and is particularly interested in colour – she dyes the cane herself. The woven paper basket shown here is made from watercolour paper. Random stripes were painted diagonally across the wet paper with watercolour inks. The paper was then cut into long strips and woven to form the box. Embroidery silks were used to create the decorative edge. *Left.*

. . . .

LISA VON CLEMM started marbling 10 years ago because of her enduring interest in paper and a sense of boredom with the decorated papers then available. At the time there were no books available and her learning period was purely experimental. Lisa marbles, using the caragheen moss method, for a three-week period in her family summer home in Maine, where the atmospheric conditions are good and she has plenty of space. Her papers are solely for her own use and most of them – marbled two to three times – have a quality of depth as a result of the layering of different colours. Lisa manipulates the colours with combs and sundry kitchen utensils and sometimes uses resist techniques. *Right.*

. . .

LISA VON CLEMM has been bookbinding for the last 15 years, although she learnt the basic techniques as a child, from her father, who was a prolific bookbinder. Her approach to bookbinding blends a modern approach with traditional methods. She bonds marbled paper shapes to leather when covering the books. This results in a decorative appearance but gives the books a 'touchable' rather than 'precious' look as she feels very strongly that beautifully bound books should be 'user friendly' and are made to be handled. The marbled papers that Lisa uses are designed and made by her for specific books. *Left.*

. . . .

A collage picture from a series, by SUSAN KINLEY. Susan studied textiles and began working with fine Japanese papers as a natural progression from delicate fabrics, such as silks. Some of the papers she uses contain silk fibres from which she makes semitransparent pieces, built from several layers. The papers and fabrics are sometimes hand-coloured, using procion dyes, watercolour and silk paints. The layered hangings or panels are made from cut or torn shapes of different densities, which are assembled into the final image. These can look most effective if they are backlit. *Left*.

· · · ·

GREGORY WARREN WILSON'S work ranges from dazzlingly brilliant to subtly pastel. The geometrical patterns are made with mosaics of papers which can be glossy, matt and/or textured, sometimes including gold leaf. They are designed to fascinate and delight the eye by balancing the symmetrical and random elements within the tightness of the plan. Gregory started using coloured papers in order to achieve the crisp straight edges not afforded by hand painting and because he wanted to work with areas of flat colour. The work is built up on graph paper, which has been sprayed with adhesive. *Right*.

· · · ·

An origami fold adapted by
PAUL JACKSON was the basis of
this paper vase, made and
designed by the author. The
vase has been made from heavy
paper specially decorated for
the purpose. The slim stencil
strips were positioned for
airbrushing, and repositioned
for each successive colour, to
give the appearance of flower
stems seen through the water in
a glass vase. *Right*.
. . . .

Candlestick-style lampbases
can be delightfully
complemented by marbled
paper shades. The shades are
made from the wide range of
papers designed by Compton
Marbling, who also market
their large selection of marbled
paper goods internationally.
Left.
. . . .

This paper jewellery includes earrings, a brooch and necklaces, all made from various decorated papers, by the author. The ideas for some of the earrings came from Florence Temko, an origami artist and published writer herself; the author is most grateful for her assistance. Paper jewellery, although of an ephemeral nature, can look most decorative. Matching sets can be specially designed to complement an outfit, and off-cuts can successfully be used to make a range of items. Jewellery-making easily becomes an addictive occupation and jewellery findings are not difficult to buy. *Left*.

. . . .

DALMA FLANDERS began decorating paper as a result of her addictive interest in the craft of bookbinding. Frustrated by the lack of suitable endpapers, she began to make her own. Dalma then decided to branch out into other fields in which she could use her decorative papers. Desk accessories have proved very successful for her and she constantly seeks new ideas to introduce to her range. She is still fascinated by the possibilities of matching and blending colours. *Left*.

. . . .

DECORATING TECHNIQUES

IN THIS SECTION, six different methods of decorating paper will be explained. These range from the very simple to the relatively complicated; whichever technique you choose, it will not take you long to produce sufficiently good results to follow the craft projects in the final section of the book.

Think about how you are going to use the paper, before you decorate it, so that the design works in the best way possible.

Consider the colour of the paper when choosing the colours you are going to work with as it will affect the final result. Test the colours on a spare piece of paper.

PASTE PAPERS
This method of decorating paper is one of the simplest and most satisfying. Designs are made by applying the paste to a block and 'printing' this on to the paper; the more common way of working is to cover the paper with the coloured paste and 'draw' an all-over design.

YOU WILL NEED:
- wallpaper paste or cornflour paste
- water-based paints
- paper, at least 100 gsm
- bowls, for the paste mixture
- brushes, for mixing colour and for brushing onto paper
- scrap paper – old newspapers
- implements to make patterns, fork, scraper, card etc
- sponges, natural and synthetic
- simple blocks, cork, string etc

Wallpaper paste is the easiest type of paste with which to work, as it is simple to mix, although the final effect may be a little coarse. If a delicate effect is required, the cornflour paste method should be used.

Mix the paste according to the directions on the packet, using a little less water than instructed – it is easy to make the paste thinner if necessary.

Add the colour and mix it in well so that there are no streaks or lumps. It is wise to test the colour on a scrap of paper to check the intensity, but remember that when it is dry it may look different.

● With the chosen paper placed on a larger piece of scrap paper, lay a trail of coloured paste along one edge of the paper and, using a wide brush, spread the paste evenly over the whole sheet.

● Draw a design into the paste with the 'comb'. It is important to work quite quickly as the paste will soon begin to dry. If the design is not satisfactory, brush over the whole thing and start again.

● There are many ways of using this method. The paste can be sponged on to the paper and, when almost dry, covered with a clean piece of lightweight paper, which is rubbed down and then peeled off.

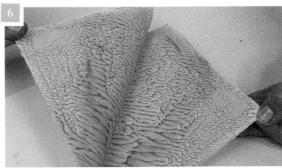

● Two sheets of paper can be covered with paste, pressed together and peeled apart. This gives a feathery, lined effect and produces two almost identical pieces of paper, which could be used for book covers.

● Another way of decorating the paper, once pasted, is to divide the sheet into squares and 'print' or 'draw' a design into the spaces. It might be advisable to use the finer cornflour paste for this method of working.

● Depending on the thickness of the paste, the patterned paper will take some time to dry and it may curl. If necessary, the paper, when quite dry, can be ironed on the wrong side or pressed flat under a pile of books.

● To make cornflour paste, mix 25g (1oz) cornflour with 50ml (2fl. oz) cold water in a saucepan and gradually stir in 150ml (generous ¼pt) boiling water. Bring to the boil, stirring constantly, and allow to boil for a minute or two. During this time, the paste will thicken steadily. It is very important that you keep stirring so that the paste is as smooth as possible. The paste will thicken as it cools: if it becomes too thick, more water can be added; sieve the mixture if it gets lumpy.

BLOCK-PRINTED PAPERS

As with the previous method, these papers can be simply produced or they can be treated in a much more complicated way. The possibilities are almost endless and a lot of pleasure can be had while experimenting. Old newspapers can be painted with ordinary household emulsion to provide an inexpensive base for trials. The papers can be designed to give an all-over pattern or they can be made in a more random style. It is quite easy to take a motif from an existing artefact and make a printing block and then to use the block to print paper to match the interior decor – but do remember that the print will be reversed when printed unless the original tracing is turned over before being cut.

There are two main methods of block printing. The simplest is to apply colour to the printing block and then press this on to the paper. Alternatively, ink can be applied to a smooth surface with a roller and the block is then pressed into the ink; finally the paper is laid over the inked area and carefully smoothed to transfer the pattern before it is lifted off and allowed to dry.

YOU WILL NEED:

- paint or ink, either oil- or water-based
- paper, 100gsm or heavier
- craft-knife
- potato
- eraser
- block of wood
- 'ink pad'
- lino
- lino-cutting tools
- piece of glass or formica
- roller
- rags and white spirit, for cleaning

Water-based colours work well with all the block materials mentioned above, except for lino with which oil-based inks are more permanent. A simple pad can be made by soaking a piece of foam in the paint and then pressing the block on to the paper. This method is practical to use with children as the mess is kept to a minimum. Depending on the final use to which the paper will be put, the background could be coloured – this can either be coloured paper or paper which has been previously painted.

The very simplest blocks can be cut from potatoes; this method is most suited to printing basic geometric shapes. Other simple objects can be used for printing, such as corks, cardboard tubes and pieces of

polystyrene. When using potatoes for block printing, a rudimentary handle can be cut in the top of the potato, so that it is easier to hold.

Two-colour patterns can be made by working two blocks at the same time. It is best to keep one block for each colour, otherwise the colours can become muddied.

● A more detailed block can be cut from an eraser, using a craft-knife. Erasers are more durable than potatoes for the purposes of block printing.

● The printing surface can be manipulated more easily if the eraser is securely glued to a wooden block.

● A more professional way of making block prints is to design a lino-cut block. This method also enables larger areas to be printed. For this purpose it is best to use specialist materials and tools. Carbon paper can be used for transferring the design prior to cutting.

● Use a roller to ink up lino blocks. First of all spread the ink on to a smooth surface and work the roller backwards and forwards and up and down, so that the roller is evenly coated.

● Next, applying uniform pressure, pass the roller over the surface of the block and lay the block on to the paper. Press the surface firmly and remove the block carefully without smudging the design on the paper. Both negative and positive shapes can be cut and a great variety of designs can be created using the two blocks together.

STENCILLED PAPERS

Stencilling is a very traditional method of decorating two–dimensional surfaces and has been used throughout the world for hundreds of years. The Japanese are particularly good at cutting extremely delicate and complicated stencils. The use of stencils was an early method of making coloured prints as a separate stencil was cut for each colour to be printed. Stencil designs are often used to create textile designs. Stencils can be made from a variety of materials and the colour can be applied to the paper using many different implements. The type of stencil to be used will depend to a great extent on the eventual use for the paper – commercial stencils of various sizes can be purchased; stencils can be cut from special waxed stencil paper, or thin card, paper or acetate can be used (card and paper are less durable when used with paints). If you are using waxed stencil paper, the cut stencil can be varnished to make it easier to clean, and, therefore, more durable.

YOU WILL NEED:
- paper from 70gsm depending on final use
- stencil material, thin card, acetate, waxed stencil paper
- craft-knife or scalpel
- felt-tipped pens or water-based paint
- sponges
- palette
- stencil brush
- airbrush

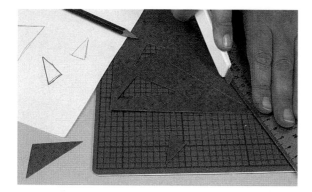

● Plan the design using ordinary paper and then transfer it to the stencil material, ready for cutting. As before, it is best to start by using simple shapes so that the potential of the method can be clearly seen.

● The method of colouring the stencilled shapes can also be done in many different ways from felt-tipped pens to sponges, stencil brushes to spray diffusers or airbrushing – each method will give a different effect. It is only through experimenting that the most appropriate or preferred method will be discovered.

Felt-tipped pens are best used for small designs or for accentuating outlines.

STENCIL BRUSHES
● When using a stencil brush, the excess paint should be removed by working on waste paper first. The brush should be used almost dry, so that the paint does not creep under the edge of the stencil and cause a blurred outline. Hold the stencil brush in a very upright position and work the paint on to the paper with a dabbing motion. Remove the stencil very carefully, so that there is no danger of smudging the area already worked. Before repositioning the stencil, make sure that the underside is clean.

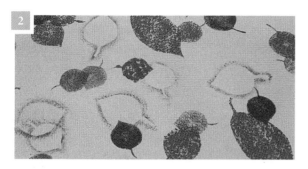

It is possible to use both parts of the stencil, either separately or together and work out a variety of patterns. An added effect can be achieved by printing the stencil on a coloured paper.

SPONGING

When using a sponge ensure that the area surrounding the cut-out shape is larger than the sponge so that the paper to be printed is protected. If this is not possible, shield the area with scrap paper. As with the stencil brush, the sponge should be used as dry as possible so that a textured effect is achieved. It will probably be necessary to have several pieces of sponge.

Two-colour effects can be created by using the same stencil twice. Allow the first colour to dry and then reposition the stencil before applying a second colour.

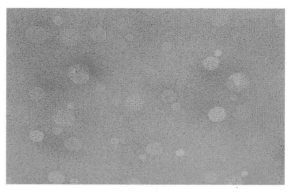

SPRAYING

A simple way to create a large piece of decorated paper is to lay strips or shapes, cut or torn from paper upon the large sheet and to spray colour over the area. The paint should be mixed to a thin consistency and used with a spray diffuser, airbrush or splattered from a stiff brush, such as a nail brush. Hold the bristles upwards and draw a piece of stiff card across the bristles towards the body so that the paint falls away on to the sheet of paper – try it first on waste paper. After repositioning the pieces of paper, a second colour could be sprayed.

REGISTRATION

If the stencil design calls for accurate registration, this can be achieved in a number of ways. A pencil line, which can later be erased, could be drawn and the stencil laid against the line. Alternatively, using an indelible pen on an acetate stencil, mark points on the second stencil, and match them with points on the first stencil.

FOLDED AND DYED PAPERS

This method originated in Japan and can be used to create some very decorative papers. It is essential to use very thin and absorbent paper; it will usually be necessary to mount the finished design on to another sheet of paper before using it in a project. Methods of mounting papers are shown later in the book in the section on basic techniques. The method requires a large working area, which should be protected with newspapers so that no accidental colouring stains occur.

YOU WILL NEED:
- absorbent paper with wet strength: lens tissue, some Japanese papers or modelspan (only available in specialist shops)
- dyes: food colours, ink or silk paints
- surgical rubber gloves
- palette
- kitchen tissue
- roller
- newspaper ● iron

The dash lines and dot dash lines indicate the folding of alternate sides of the paper necessary to give accordion pleating.

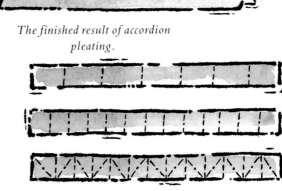

The finished result of accordion pleating.

These four diagrams show different variations of accordion pleating.

● When the paper has been folded into a small package, it is ready to be dyed. The dyes, whichever type has been chosen, should be dispensed into small, stable open containers. Holding the package tightly, dip each corner or edge. Depending on the absorbency of the paper, the colour will spread and this is how the patterns are created.

● Now lay the paper on some waste newspaper and partially unfold it. Cover the pleated strip with another piece of paper and apply pressure, either with the hand or with a roller to absorb excess moisture from the paper and stop the colour spreading any further.

● The next step is the most hazardous, as the wet paper is fragile and needs careful handling. Lift the pleated paper and unfold it. Then lay it out to dry on a piece of newspaper. Wear surgical rubber gloves if you do not want to stain your fingers and nails – they will not hamper dexterity.

● When the paper is quite dry, it can be ironed gently. The pleat lines will always show and should be regarded as part of the design.

TIPS

● If the paper package is dampened before dyeing, the absorbency will be increased and the resulting pattern will have a softer appearance.

● One colour can be used in different strengths and this can create a very subtle effect.

● It is not essential to dye the whole sheet: some areas can be left white as part of the design.

LAMINATED PAPERS

This method is original, unorthodox and totally experimental but produces interesting and unusual effects. The idea originated from 'plant' papers, which are increasingly popular papers available in specialist shops. In traditional 'plant' papers, the flowers are added during the making of the paper.

YOU WILL NEED:
● base paper, 70 to 140 gsm
● top paper, very lightweight
● pressed flowers or paper bits
● thinned PVA adhesive or fusible webbing
● iron

● Decide on the size of paper to be laminated, and cut both the base and the top sheet slightly oversize. Lay the base sheet on some waste paper, brush all over with thinned PVA and leave to dry.

● Lay the flowers, which have been pressed well ahead of time, or paper bits, in the required position on the glued paper.

● Place the top sheet over the base sheet, cover it with a thin piece of waste paper, and iron it carefully with a warm to hot iron.

● If you are using a fusible webbing, iron it on to the base sheet, peel the backing away and lay the pieces in place before sandwiching them by ironing the other sheet on top. As the top paper is very thin, it is advisable to place a piece of silicone release or greaseproof paper between the top paper and the iron so that none of the adhesive is accidentally transferred to the bottom of the iron.

MARBLED PAPERS

Marbled papers are probably the most widely known of decorated papers and these days they are used for embellishing a great number of objects, from desk accessories to furniture and furnishings. Marbled papers were originally used almost exclusively by bookbinders.

The technique has existed, in its various forms, for hundreds of years. The decoration is achieved by floating colours on a liquid surface and drawing patterns through the colours before transferring them to a piece of paper or other material. The process as we know it today is thought to have been invented in eastern Europe, but much of the history is hazy and surrounded by secrecy, as is the technique itself. It was not unusual for apprentices to be taught only a certain number of the stages, so that they could not pass on any useful information to rival producers. Even to this day, there is a certain guardedness among some marblers.

There are three recognized methods of marbling – from simple to complex and, inevitably, the most complicated method offers the greatest control. Only two are described here, the most complex – using caragheen moss and watercolours – being omitted. The methods below involve oil colours, and widely available materials and equipment. These ways of marbling can be attempted, with satisfactory results, and even if you have no experience at all you will soon develop the skill to control your designs.

METHOD 1

The first method of marbling is simple, produces pleasing results very quickly, and requires the minimum of equipment. However, it is essential to cover the work area with newspapers or some other protective covering as the paints being used are oil-based and will leave marks, which although removable, can stain.

YOU WILL NEED:
- paper, 90 to 120gsm
- dish – roasting tin or photographer's tray
- student quality oil paints
- white spirit or turpentine
- jars for colours
- brushes for mixing
- newspaper strips for cleaning
- medicine droppers
- sticks and straws
- empty box for rubbish

Prepare everything before starting to work on the papers. Fill the tray with water and allow it to settle at room temperature. Choose two or more colours and mix each separately with the white spirit or turpentine. The consistency should be even and quite thin – the colour should drop easily from the brush when tapped against the side of the tray. When the colour lands on the surface of the water it should disperse over the area. If this does not happen then the colour should be diluted with more white spirit, dropped on to the water and tested again. If the colour still does not spread, the temperature of the water may be wrong. If the colour disperses too much, it is probably too thin and more oil paint should be added.

When the colours have been mixed to the correct consistency, the surface of the water should be skimmed with the newspaper strips. Newspaper should be torn into strips the width of the tray and about 7cm (3in) deep. The wet and stained strips of newspaper should then be dropped into a strategically placed empty rubbish box.

The sheets of paper should be cut so that they are slightly smaller than the tray. Prepare several sheets (perhaps choosing different colours), so that once marbling has started the process can be continuous.

● Dip the brush in the diluted colour and allow drops to fall on the surface of the water. Alternatively, use a medicine dropper to put the colour on the water in a more controlled way.

● When the surface is evenly covered, the colours can be swirled with a stick or blown with a straw so that a loose pattern is created. Work quite quickly so that the colours do not mix too much and become muddied.

● Take a piece of paper and, holding it at diagonally opposite corners, lower it, with a rolling movement, on to the surface of the water. Take care to do this smoothly so that no air bubbles are trapped between the paper and the water.
Skim the surface of the water with newspaper strips again before starting another design.

● When the paper is flat on the water, let go and prepare to pick it up. Take hold of two adjacent corners, preferably on the long side, and lift up. Allow the water to drip off for a moment and then lay the paper, patterned side up, on a few sheets of newspaper to dry.

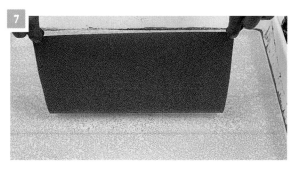

● A single colour pattern on a coloured background paper can look very effective.

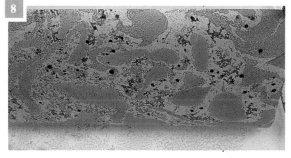

● Patterns can also be created using two or more colours on white or toning paper.

METHOD 2

The second method of marbling is a little more complicated but allows a greater degree of control. Much enjoyment can be had while experimenting with the method and usable papers will result quite quickly. The trial-and-error approach is one of the best ways of learning.

It requires a little more equipment than the previous method, as the oil colours are floated on a bath of size, which allows the drops to be positioned. Ox-gall is added to the colours and acts as a dispersant by breaking the surface tension of the size. Again, it is essential to cover your work surface with some form of protection – the paints being used are oil-based and may leave stain marks. As with the previous method, it is best to organize everything in advance in a methodical way. Prepare the size, dilute the oil paints, cut up the strips of newspaper and prepare the sheets to be marbled.

YOU WILL NEED:

- paper, 90 to 120gsm
- dish – roasting tin or photographer's tray
- wallpaper paste
- mixing bowl or bucket
- sieve
- student quality oil paints
- white spirit or turpentine
- ox-gall
- jars for colours
- brushes
- newspaper strips
- medicine droppers
- sticks and combs
- empty box for rubbish
- thick card
- double-sided sticky tape
- long pins
- ruler
- pencil

● The size is prepared in the following way. Use approximately one heaped tablespoon of wallpaper paste powder to 1 litre (2 pints) of lukewarm water. Mix so that the resulting solution is smooth – if necessary it can be sieved before being poured into the tray. It is best to err on the side of thickness as the size can always be thinned. It is much more difficult to thicken the size smoothly.

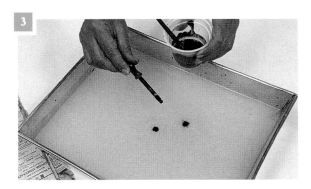

● When the size and the oil colours are ready, the ox-gall can be added. This step is the most difficult as each colour thins and reacts differently to the ox-gall and is also affected by the temperature of the room and the size bath.

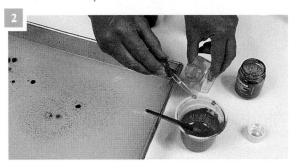

● Add the ox-gall drop by drop with the medicine dropper. Start by adding about eight drops to three teaspoons of colour, mix well and test. A drop of colour on the surface of the size should spread into a regular circle about 2.5 cm (1in) in diameter. If it does not spread, add more ox-gall and try again. If the colour spreads too far and too thinly, there is probably too much ox-gall and more thinned oil paint could be added. If the colour sinks or does not spread, it may be that the size is too thick and water should be stirred in carefully. The size should be at approximately room-temperature, assuming there is no heat wave.

Skim the surface of the size with newspaper torn into strips the width of the tray and about 7cm (3in) deep. Throw the used strips away.

● Now decorate a piece of paper. Load the brush with colour and splatter drops on to the surface of the size by tapping the handle of the brush against the edge of the tray. Repeat with a second or third colour, if wished.

Patterns can be drawn on the size with a stick or knitting needle pulled gently and slowly through the colours. Try to work on the surface of the size so that as little disturbance as possible is caused. When the pattern is satisfactory, it can be transferred to the paper.

● Take a piece of paper and, holding it at diagonally opposite corners, lower it on to the surface of the size. Try to do this with a smooth rolling movement so that no air bubbles become trapped between the paper and the size, as they would cause unwanted and unattractive white spaces in the finished design.

When the paper is flat on the surface of the size, prepare to pick it up by taking hold of two adjacent corners, preferably on the long side. Lift it in a peeling motion. Allow the excess size to run off the paper before laying it, patterned side up, on a few sheets of newspaper to dry. If the size is very thick, the paper can be gently rinsed. Skim the surface of the water with newspaper strips to clean it again before starting another design.

● More regular designs can be made with this method but the colours may need some adjustment. The ox-gall, which allows the colours to spread, will be needed in greater quantities for each successive colour. It is, therefore, necessary to decide on the colour combination before starting, and to check the dispersal of colours.

● This method of working is the way to create sets of designs, as it is possible to make notes about the positioning of the drops of colour and the style of the manipulation, either with sticks or combs.

MARBLING COMBS
● It is possible to buy marbling combs, but they can easily be made in a variety of sizes.

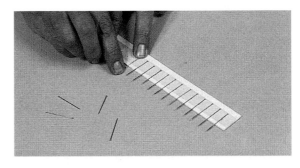

● Cut two strips of card a little narrower than the tray and 5cm (2in) deep. Mark the card at regular intervals eg every 0.5cm (¼in) and then lay a strip of double-sided tape along one edge of the card.
● Place long pins on the tape at the marked points so that they protrude about 1cm (½in). Stick double-sided tape to the second piece of card and press the two pieces together.
● Varnish the comb or wrap it in plastic film to make it more durable.

Pencil

Set square

Pencil

MATERIALS AND EQUIPMENT

THROUGHOUT THE BOOK the main material used is paper. This apparently unexciting material comes in many different guises and it is important that you understand some of its basic qualities if you are going to select the most appropriate type for the project in hand.

The papers used in this book have been purchased, although paper-making is a craft that can be easily learnt. Most of the papers required for the projects can be readily found in ordinary art shops and those projects that require specialist papers can often be worked with alternative papers. Some specialist shops selling papers offer a mail order service.

Paper and card have two important properties – weight and grain. Paper weight is measured in grams per square metre, abbreviated to g/m^2 or gsm. Occasionally the weight is given in pounds per ream – a ream is 500 sheets regardless of dimensions. Lightweight papers include tissue paper, lens tissue and many of the handmade Japanese papers, which are so beautiful and surprisingly strong. As a guideline, papers in daily use, such as writing paper, weigh between 80gsm and 120gsm and would be classed as light- to medium-weight. Papers from 150gsm to 200gsm are medium- to heavyweight and anything over 225gsm is card. When the weight goes up to 500gsm, the material is known as board. Confusingly, card and board are sometimes measured by their thickness in micrometres, rather than by weight.

The grain defines the direction in which the fibres of the paper lie. Handmade paper has no grain, but all other paper made on moulds using moving belts does; the fibres settle in the direction in which the belt is moving. For most of the projects in this book it is important that the paper's grain is taken into account.

Grain imparts certain qualities to paper. The paper can be torn, curved, folded or creased more readily along than across its grain; paper with grain, when wetted with water or adhesive can fall apart or dry unevenly and curl or wrinkle. To stop this happening dampen the paper on both sides and leave it to dry under pressure.

Paper has many other properties which are created in the making of the material. Coloured paper is created by the addition of pigment to the paper pulp before it settles on the mesh. The paper can also be textured in manufacture, by the addition of fibres or the use of rollers. These rollers affect the finished appearance of the paper and can make its surface rough, ultra-smooth or something in between. The absorbency of paper can also be controlled during manufacture by the addition of size, made from gelatine or starch.

Paper is available in many sizes and there are various standards. However, the sizes most widely known are the A sizes – from A1 to A6. It is possible to find smaller sizes but these six are the most usual. A1 is 84 × 59cm (33 × 23½in); A2 is half of this measurement ie 42 × 59cm (16½ × 23½in) and so on down to A6, 15 × 10.5cm (6 × 4in). If the grain runs down the long measurement of one size of paper, it will often run the short measurement of the next size down, as it will have been cut from the same roll of manufactured paper. It is possible to purchase rolls of paper but inevitably this means buying large quantities. However, it

How to find the grain direction in paper

grain direction

Folding across the grain

grain direction

grain direction

Folding with the grain

CAT. NO. 0411.05

Steel rule/ cutting edge

Pencil sharpener

Paper

Eraser

Scalpel

X-acto knife

A variety of scissors

Cutting mat

Card

does mean that large projects, such as printing hand-blocked wallpaper, can be considered.

Adhesive is another important material used in the projects. The best adhesive is the one with which you feel most comfortable. Three main types have been used in the book: PVA adhesive, which has many other names (each signifying only slight differences in quality) such as school glue, white glue and some types of paint medium; spray adhesive, which should be used sparingly in a well-ventilated area; impact adhesive allows for the exact positioning of the two pieces to be joined – a thin layer of glue is trailed along the two edges to be joined and allowed to dry for a short time before the two glued edges are brought together: this adhesive makes very strong bonds. Fusible webbing, available from haberdashery departments and supplied with instructions for use, will bond two separate and dissimilar materials together.

BASIC TECHNIQUES

THIS SECTION aims to cover the basic techniques which will recur later in the book.

MEASURING AND CUTTING PAPER OR CARD

Lay the paper or card on the cutting mat or waste card and, working from a straight cut edge – if necessary cut off a strip of paper before starting – measure the required distance from the edge and, with a sharp pencil, make a mark. Move the ruler down the sheet of paper or card, measure again and make another mark.

If the line is only to be drawn, then turn the sheet through 90° and lay the ruler so that the two marks, just made, can be joined.

If the paper or card is to be cut, the previous step could be omitted and, when the metal ruler or straight-edge has been laid in position, the sheet can be cut with a craft-knife. It is best to use a craft-knife when cutting straight lines and good results will soon be achieved after a little practice.

SCORING

This technique is very useful and will help give a professional appearance to the completed project as all folds or creases will have a crisp finish. The aim of scoring a piece of paper or card is to open up one side so that it will bend more easily.

The line is usually scored, with a bone folder or the back of a craft-knife or scissor blade, on the outside of the work – the paper is bent away from the line. Needless to say, there are exceptions and scoring is less important if you are using thin paper: note that it may be easier to crease the paper, after scoring, against the ruler while it is still in position. However, care should be taken not to score the sheet too deeply and inadvertently create two sheets.

When scoring card, it is necessary to cut through half the thickness of the card. This has to be very carefully gauged and it is advisable to practise first on a scrap piece of the same card.

Scoring is great fun and need not be done in straight lines. Paper can be scored in curves and or on both sides alternately to give attractive raised surfaces.

BOX-MAKING

There are two main methods of making boxes. The first method can be used for small to medium-sized boxes from one piece of lightweight card; the second is for boxes of any size made from board, which are constructed from cut pieces glued together. Accuracy is needed for both methods but apart from that, no special skills are necessary.

METHOD 1

● In this example a small rectangular box is shown. First the plan of the box is drawn – work out all the dimensions carefully. If you are going to cover the box with decorated paper, do this before you glue it together. If you are making the box from decorated card, calculate the fall of the decorative pattern before drawing the plan, especially if using an all-over pattern. Alternatively, design your stencil or block prints to fit the box.

● Draw the plan using the measuring method described previously and always check that the angles are 90°. Glue flaps should be added to the basic plan. These should be at least 1cm (½in) deep, but the bigger the box, the deeper the glue flaps must be. Check that there are the correct number of glue flaps: there should be the same number of edges with flaps as without. The flaps used to close the box, tucking flaps, can be deeper and more sharply angled to give a tighter fit.

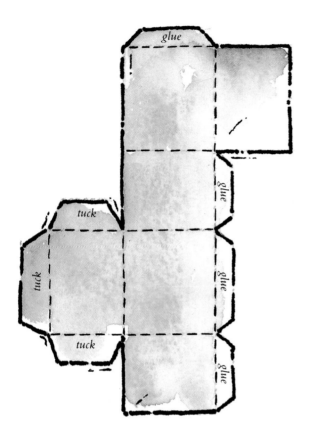

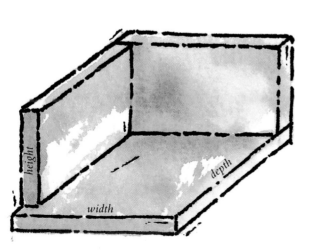

● Cut out the shape, using a craft-knife or scalpel. Take care when cutting the glue flaps not to cut into the work accidentally. Always cut away from the work when removing small waste pieces.

Score all the uncut lines and bend the box into shape. Check that everything fits neatly prior to glueing.

METHOD 2

The first thing to decide is what size you want the box to be. Remember that since the box is constructed by glueing the edges together, you need to take into account the thickness of the board. Therefore two sides will be the required width, and the other two sides will be the required width less the two board thicknesses. The size of the base must also take the thickness of the board into account. If you wish to make a lid, work out its size as if making another box to fit the box but with a considerably reduced height.

● In order to get good results, use good quality board – special board can be purchased (grey board or mill board) or the stiff card backs of drawing pads can be used. In some of the projects the board can be left unlined, as the inside of the box will not show, but as a general rule, it is best to cover both sides of the board so that the 'pull' exerted by the glue used to cover the outside will be equal inside and out, and not distort the box one way or the other.

● Once you have decided on the dimensions for the box, mark out the measurements on the board and cut out all the pieces. If the box is to be lined, do it now following the method below. Before you glue the pieces together, check that there are no rough edges – rub them off with glasspaper if necessary. It is also wise to check that all the pieces fit accurately.

● Now, using impact adhesive, run a thin trail of glue along the two outer edges of the side pieces and along the two corresponding cut edges of the other pieces.

● Leave to dry for 10 minutes and then carefully press the pieces together.

● Using the above method, stick the base in position. When the box has had time to set, check that the joins are flush and, if necessary, sand until even.

COVERING WITH PAPER

Accuracy is again an important factor. When covering any article with paper, it is always advisable to check the properties of the paper you are using – some papers will stretch when wetted with glue. There are alternative ways of fixing paper to board. In most instances glue is spread on paper which is then positioned on the piece to be covered. An exception to this might be when covering board for the lining of a box. When covering a two-dimensional object, it will usually be necessary to allow turnings on all sides of the paper – these should be about 1.5cm (¾in) depending on the thickness of the board. When covering a three-dimensional object, turnings are necessary only on some edges. When covering board for lining boxes, the edges will be cut flush.

TO COVER A TWO-DIMENSIONAL OBJECT

● Cut an oversize piece of paper and lightly mark the position of the board on the wrong side of the paper. Then trim the edges so that the turnings are the right size. Cut diagonally across the corners, allowing for the thickness of the board, so that the corners will be neatly mitred when turned in.

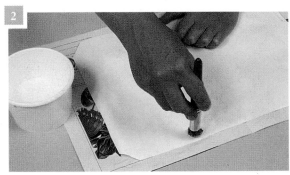

● Lay the trimmed paper on a sheet of waste paper and brush all over with adhesive.

● Carefully lift up the glued paper to remove the waste sheet and lay on the piece of board, smoothing it out gently with your hand to ensure there are no air bubbles.

● Working quite quickly, turn the board so that the covered side lies on the clean work surface, and the edges can now be turned over. If the adhesive has dried too much, more can be carefully brushed on to the turnings. Leave to dry under a little pressure, if possible.

● Detail of a completed corner.

TO COVER A THREE-DIMENSIONAL OBJECT

It is a little more complicated to work out the size of the paper for this type of covering, but the glueing process is the same. It is useful to have some long strips of lightweight paper to help assess the size required. It is also helpful to draw out a rough sketch. In the example, a box is shown, but tubes or other geometric shapes can be covered equally effectively using the same method.

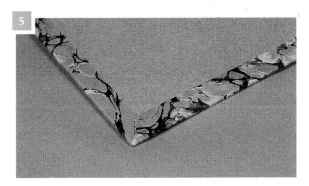

● Using a strip of paper, lay it around the box, firmly creasing all the corners and allowing for turnings at the top. Take another strip of paper and measure around the other dimension. These two strips, laid flat, will give the overall size of the piece of paper needed to cover the object.

● It is now possible to draw the plan on the wrong side of the paper, making sure that all the lines and all the angles are really accurate. Before cutting, lay the object on the paper and, holding the paper around it, check that it is absolutely correct. Then add glue flaps and cut out.

When sticking the paper to the object it is easier to do it in stages, first the base and then the sides with the glue flaps, followed by the remaining sides and finally, in the case of a container, the top edge and turnings. If the paper is very thick it can be dampened slightly with a sponge, prior to being brushed with adhesive, to make it more flexible.

If you are covering a container that has not already been lined, the turnings could be taken to the bottom and a piece of paper then glued on to the bottom to give a neat finished appearance.

MOUNTING PAPER ON TO PAPER OR CARD

In some instances it is necessary to mount very light-weight paper on to another sheet of paper or card, in order to be able to use it for a further project. A good example would be the folded and dyed paper technique explained in the earlier Decorating Techniques section.

Mounting such papers on other base materials gives them greater stability and renders them less delicate; but the technique needs to be carefully executed and certain rules need to be observed. The most important rule refers to the grain of the paper: it is essential that the grain of both materials runs in the same direction. If it does not, the papers will not dry flat because the grain in them will pull the papers across each other. It is also important that paper is not made too wet by the adhesive as this will cause the pasted sheet of paper to stretch and will again result in the finished piece not drying flat. It is always advisable to test papers and adhesives before starting on a given project. As with other basic techniques, there are several methods of working. The two methods described here are the least messy and although the two papers can be stuck together as soon as the glue has been brushed on, it takes practice not to get wrinkles in the paper, especially if the paper is very thin.

METHOD 1

Take the two sheets and lay them side by side on a clean working surface with the right sides of the papers facing downwards. Then apply PVA adhesive quickly and evenly across one whole sheet of paper. The adhesive should be brushed on to the heavier of the two papers.

Allow the adhesive to dry and then place the lighter weight paper in position on top, right side up. Using a piece of waste paper as protection, iron the whole area with a warm to hot iron. The heat will reactivate the adhesive and the two sheets of paper will be bonded together.

METHOD 2

If you are using extremely thin or delicate papers, it is sometimes almost impossible to spread the adhesive. Fusible webbing, available from haberdashery departments, is the ideal material for this purpose. It is very fine and is sold with a paper backing.

Lay the fusible webbing, rough side down, on the wrong side of one sheet of paper and iron in place.

Peel away the backing sheet and place the second sheet of paper, right side uppermost, on top. Cover it with a protective sheet of waste paper and iron with a warm iron so that the papers are fused together. This adhesive may not be suitable for valuable papers that need conservation materials.

GLOSSARY

Acetate A thin film of transparent plastic, which can be used to make a stencil.

Airbrush An atomizer, using compressed air, to spray paint on to a surface.

Album A book of blank pages for keeping photographs, postcards or drawings.

Block A piece of wood or other material, which can be carved to create a relief surface for printing.

Bone folder A tool used by bookbinders and leather workers to fold and crease material accurately and smoothly.

Bookcloth Finely woven material, sometimes paper-backed and/or coated with a sealant, used to cover books.

Caragheen moss Dried seaweed used in the making of a type of size used for classic paper marbling.

Crease A mark made by folding.

Emulsion A type of water-soluble household paint.

Endpapers Folded sheets of paper, often decorated, stuck inside the front and back covers of books.

Fusible webbing A fine adhesive web on a paper backing, which when ironed enables two materials to be bonded together.

Glasspaper A paper, coated with a fine abrasive material, used for smoothing wood and other surfaces.

Grain The alignment of the fibrous materials in sheets of paper.

Hinge A form of join, enabling two parts of the same unit to bend.

Indelible Permanent, as in a marker pen.

Laminate Two layers of paper bonded together, either to enclose a decorative substance or for strengthening.

Lino-cut A design carved in relief from a piece of linoleum.

Marbling An ancient technique of decorating paper with patterns that look like marble.

Masking tape An adhesive tape which can be used to hold things in place temporarily.

Mitre A diagonal join where the turnings on two sides meet at the corner.

Mould The frame, used in paper-making, across which a mesh is stretched and on which the pulp then forms the sheet of paper.

Mount 1. To fix to a backing. 2. The piece of paper or card that surrounds a picture or photograph.

Origami The Japanese art of creating objects from folded paper.

Ox-gall An agent, which when added to water, decreases the surface tension.

Paste A mixture, made from starch, cornflour or cellulose, with water, which acts as the binder for the colour used in creating paste decorated papers. It is also a form of adhesive.

Pleat Folds formed by doubling material back on itself.

Portfolio A flat case used for holding papers.

Pulp The moist mixture of fibres from which paper is made.

Registration The alignment of two or more stencils or blocks, necessary when printing more than one colour.

Roller The cylinder on an axle with a handle which is used to spread paint or ink.

Score To mark a fold line without cutting through the material so as to allow the material to be bent.

Screwbinder Two threaded components which, when fastened, hold papers together.

Silicone release A paper coated with silicone to which nothing will stick.

Size A substance made from a variety of ingredients such as starch, gelatine, cellulose or caragheen moss. It can also be added to paper pulp to make the paper less absorbent. Colours can be floated on a size solution for paper marbling.

Spine The back of a book or portfolio.

Spray diffuser A tool which enables colour to be dispersed finely over a wide area.

Stencil A thin sheet from which designs have been cut out so that colour can be applied through the open area to the surface below.

Turpentine substitute A thinner and solvent for use with oil-based paints. It is highly flammable and should be used with care. It is also called white spirit.

WRITING PAPER
AND GREETINGS CARDS

THESE SATISFYING but relatively simple projects can be designed and made for your own use or for other people. The writing paper, whether purchased or made by cutting up large pieces of paper, is best decorated with stencilling or block printing, and can be personalized with initials or a motif.

Greetings cards can be designed for all occasions and used as notelets for short letters. You can make a card from a single fold, well scored, in lightweight card (about 150gsm) on to the front of which you then stick a decorated piece of paper. A good paper, carefully cut, and an attractive design neatly executed can add up to an expensive-looking and professional finished result.

~

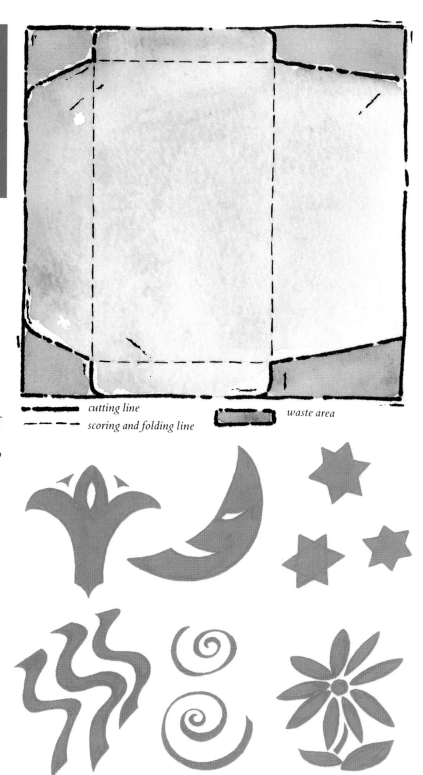

> **MATERIALS AND EQUIPMENT**
> ● *Basic equipment* ● *selected papers* ● *stencil and/or block material* ● *paint and/or printing ink*
> . . . . . .

WRITING PAPER

TIP

When decorating stationery, always work in an organized way with plenty of space because you will probably have to lay the printed sheets out to dry.

If you are designing your own writing paper, make matching envelopes too – fold in the side flaps, put glue on the side edges of the bottom flap and fold it up and stick it in place, turn down the top flap and seal, either with glue or double-sided adhesive tape.
A lining, made from a folded and dyed paper could be added before the envelope is glued.

In these examples, stencilling and block printing have been used. Some of the examples use commercial stencils or blocks but, as has been shown in the previous section, stencils and blocks can be designed and made without much problem.

cutting line

scoring and folding line

waste area

STENCILLED PATTERNS

For stencilled patterns, try to use transparent stencil material so that the stencil can be correctly positioned, particularly if more than one colour is being used. It is also possible, when using two or more colours, to make location marks on the stencil for the second or subsequent colour.

First design and cut the stencils and test them on some spare paper.

When positioning the stencil on the sheet of paper, it is a good idea to draw a faint pencil line, which can be erased, or to tape a strip of paper, in a contrasting colour, against which the stencil can be aligned.

As stencils for writing paper are usually fairly small it is quite a good idea to use felt-tipped pens to draw the image.

BLOCK-PRINTED PATTERNS

If the method of decorating the writing paper is to be block printing, then the block can be cut from any of the materials shown in the previous section. The simplest is the potato block, but this can be used for a short time only, although a print can be taken and the block re-cut on a subsequent occasion. A more permanent block can be cut from an eraser.

Block printing with potato blocks and water-based paints is an extremely spontaneous way of printing and it is easy to print a large quantity of writing paper very quickly. A faint pencil line can be drawn as a guideline for the placing of the prints, particularly if the design runs along one edge of the paper. If you are working with two colours, apply the second colour as you did the first after the first colour has dried.

Once you have cut the block and prepared the paint, work in a methodical way. Print the paper and then lay it out to dry. Try to overlap the sheets in such a way that they take up the minimum of space, but do not smudge each other.

MATERIALS AND EQUIPMENT

● *Basic equipment* ●
lightweight card ● *marbled,*
or other decorated, paper ●
adhesive ● *purchased card*
(optional) ● *very*
lightweight top paper ●
thinned PVA or fusible
webbing ● *pressed flowers*
or paper pieces ● *iron*
● *double-sided adhesive tape*
· · · · · ·

GREETING CARDS

TIP

Consider the size of readily
available envelopes before making
your own cards. Although it is
easy to make envelopes, it is
very time-consuming to make
too many.

1 The card should be cut so that,
when folded, it measures 0.5–
1cm (⅜–½in) less than the envelope
in the length and width. The card
will fold best if the grain runs in the
same direction as the fold (see Basic
Techniques).

2 Now take the decorated paper
and select an area from it to be
stuck on the front of the card. Some
designs will need a wider border
than others; you will have to
establish the correct width by trial
and error, because experiments
with small pieces will not provide
the information, as the balance will
vary with the size of the card. Start
with a relatively large piece and, if
the border looks too narrow, trim
the decorated paper a little until the
design is balanced. When the
appearance of the card is
satisfactory, glue the decorated
paper piece into place.

3 Cut a piece of card the same length as the envelope to be used and three times as wide. Score the card and fold it into three equal parts. Now prepare the aperture in the following way. Decide on the shape and size of the opening to be cut in the central part of the card. Cards with oval or similar shaped apertures are available in crafts shops. With the folds facing upwards, prepare the left-hand side of the card using either one of the methods of laminating papers (see page 23). Lay the flat paper pieces or pressed flowers in position on the glued surface and cover with tissue, which has been cut to size. Iron the tissue in place.

4 Complete the card by sticking down the aperture over the laminated design. This can be done either with glue spread carefully around the outer edges of the opening or with double-sided adhesive tape.

NOTELET CASE

THIS IS an ideal way of presenting writing paper or notelet cards, which have been decorated using techniques shown in other projects. The example shown here is made from a folded and dyed paper mounted on to lightweight card, about 150gsm. However, card decorated in other ways could be used. Accuracy is of the utmost importance when making this project so that the case looks neat and closes properly. Study the diagram carefully before you start.

~

**MATERIALS
AND EQUIPMENT**

● *Basic equipment* ●
decorated card ● *bone folder*
● *small coin* ● *suitable*
adhesive

· · · · · ·

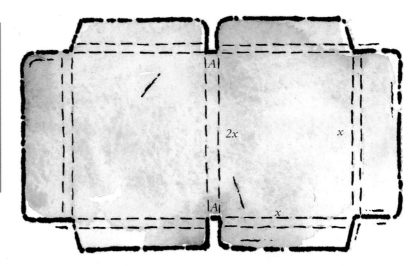

Draw the diagram lightly on the wrong side of the decorated card. The dimensions can be altered to suit the requirements of the paper or cards to be contained in the finished wallet. The diagram shows the proportions of the wallet: the long flap, forming the pocket, is deeper than the flaps at the top and the bottom; the space in the middle 'A' is twice as wide (2x) as the spaces scored around the outer edges (x), so that, when closed, both sides of the wallet are accommodated.

Use a small coin to draw curves at the exposed corners.

1 Cut out the wallet around the solid lines. Where possible cut away from the work – especially at the inner corners – if the knife slips, it is all too easy to cut into the work.

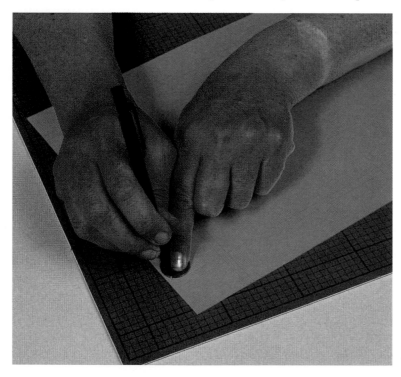

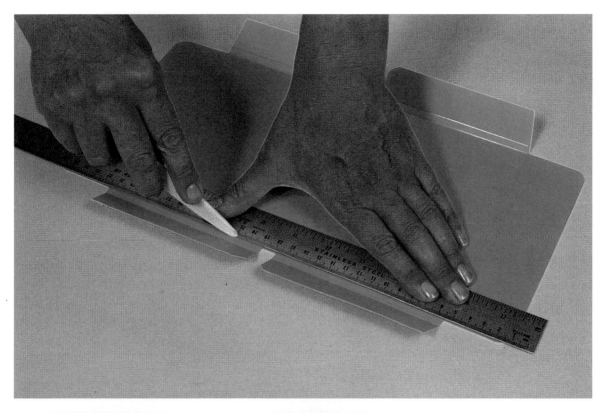

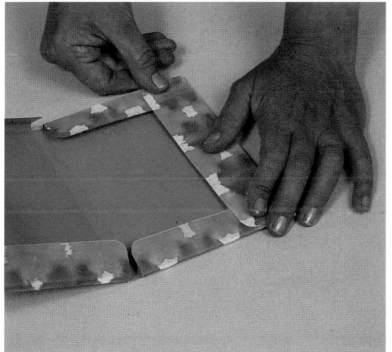

2 Score all the dotted lines with the bone folder.

Working from the outer edges, fold up the scored lines and crease firmly into position. Check that the corners are square and meet neatly.

3 Apply adhesive to the corners of the long flaps, which overlap the top and bottom flaps. Stick in position and hold for a few minutes until the glue is dry.

GIFT BAGS

BAGS MADE from paper are simple to make and can be made in any number of sizes, using lightweight paper; the larger the bag, the heavier the paper should be. If the bag is quite large or for carrying heavy items, such as bottles, its base and handles should be reinforced with card. Handles can be made from toning ribbons or yarns, and gift tags can be made to match.

~

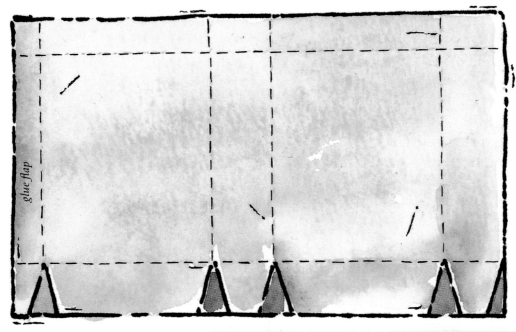

glue flap

—— *cutting line*

----- *scoring and folding line*

▭ *waste area*

TIP

Before starting to make a bag there are a few things to remember. When you draw the plan for the bag, ensure that all the angles are right angles (90°) so that the bag will be square when finished and will stand straight. The base flaps should be about 1cm (½in) less than the width of the sides of the bag. When making up the bag, score all the fold lines so that they will crease easily and crisply, particularly when using heavier paper.

MATERIALS AND EQUIPMENT

● *Basic equipment ●
selected decorated paper ●
adhesive ● ribbon or yarn
for handles*

· · · · · ·

1 Draw the plan on the reverse side of the paper, so that none of the working lines shows on the outside when the bag is folded and finished. Cut out the shape, removing the waste areas.

Score and crease all the lines. Stick down the top flap, using a suitable adhesive. This adds strength and gives a neat finished appearance.

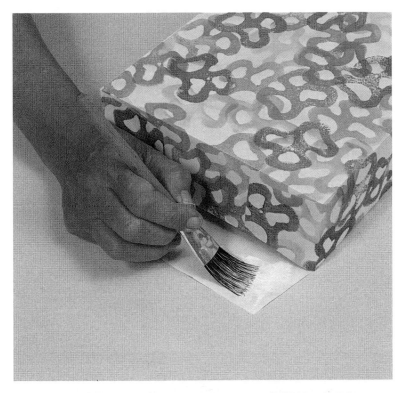

2 Now stick the glue flap to the side – again this gives a neater appearance as the join is almost invisible at the side.

Next, stick the base flaps to each other. Apply adhesive to the wrong side of the side flaps and stick them to the back flap. Then apply adhesive to the wrong side of the front flap and stick this down.

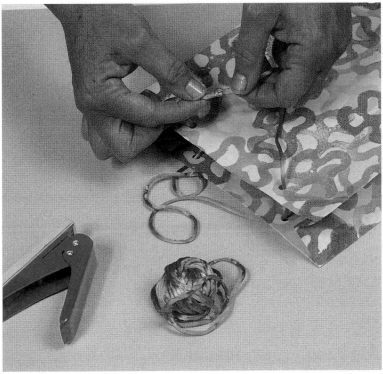

3 Finally, make holes for the handles through the double thickness at the top edge, and thread the chosen ribbon or yarn through these holes. There are various methods of threading – some ways are purely decorative and others actually serve to fasten the bag shut.

BOX COVER

THIS IDEA greatly enhances the appearance of an ordinary item and can make it suitable as a gift. The card cover in this example has been made to fit a box of tissues. The lightweight card has been airbrushed using self-adhesive dots as stencils. The method used here is based on the first method described for box-making in the Basic Techniques section. As the cover slips over the tissue box, it will not be necessary to incorporate a lid and tucking flap in the basic plan.

~

MATERIALS AND EQUIPMENT

● *Basic equipment* ●
airbrushed lightweight card
● *scrap card for template*
● *quick-drying adhesive*
· · · · · ·

TIP
It is important to take accurate measurements so that the cover slips snugly over the tissue box when finished. The measuring can be done either with a strip of paper, or the sides and top can be measured and added together.

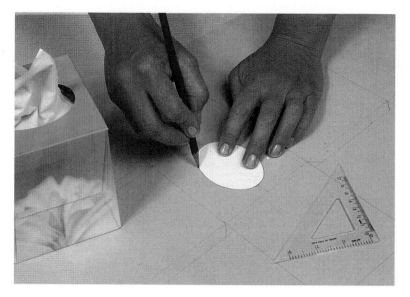

1 Draw the plan on the wrong side of the prepared card and add the glue flaps, 1cm (⅜in) deep, to two sides of the plan.
  Make a template of the hole in the top of the box, through which the tissues are pulled. Place this template carefully in the middle of the top of the plan, draw around it and cut it out.

2 Now cut out the plan, using a sharp blade, so that there is no danger of a ragged-looking edge when cutting through the card. Score along all the lines and fold up.

3 Check the fit of the cover before glueing. If all is well, apply adhesive to the glue flaps and hold in position over the tissue box while the glue sets. Be careful not to apply too much adhesive to the glue flaps, because excess adhesive may ooze out and cause the cover to stick to the tissue box.

4 The cover is now completed but could be further embellished by the addition of a toning braid, either purchased or handmade. This could be glued around the lower edge and would make the bottom of the cover stronger.

WASTEPAPER CONTAINER

THE WASTEPAPER container shown is a simple idea, but the decoration can make a great difference to a mundane item. It is possible to cover a purchased round wastepaper tub (rather than making one from scratch). The decoration can be chosen to complete or complement a set of desk accessories. A wastepaper container that has been bought will not need lining but will almost certainly require trimming at the top and bottom to cover the manufacturer's finish; the trim can consist of a matching braid or paper plait.

~

MATERIALS AND EQUIPMENT

● *Basic equipment* ● *thick card* ● *decorated paper for covering* ● *toning paper for lining* ● *impact adhesive* ● *PVA adhesive*
. . . . . .

Decide upon the size of the container to be made – this may be influenced by the amount of decorated paper you have available. Most wastepaper tubs are about 25cm (10in) high and 20cm (8in) across the opening, but these dimensions are totally variable.

1 Cut the card into the correct number of pieces of the required size and line with the toning paper (see Basic Techniques section).

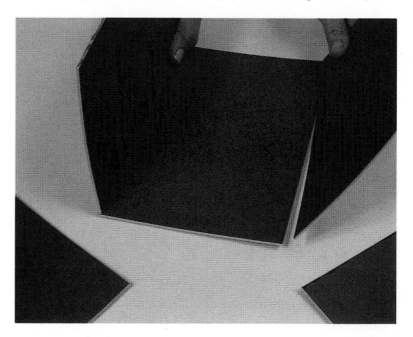

2 Using the impact adhesive, stick the sides together. When this has dried, stick the base to the sides and make sure that the edges are as smooth as possible. It will be necessary to pay attention to this point as the card will probably be a little curved, due to the 'pull' of the adhesive already used for lining the inside.

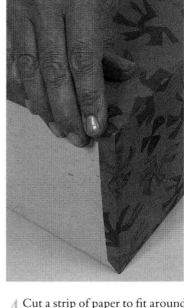

3 The most economical way to cover the container is to cover the base and then to wrap a strip around the sides. Cut a piece of the decorated paper which is at least 1cm (⅜in) larger on all sides than the base of the wastepaper tub. Apply adhesive to this piece of paper and stick it to the card, smoothing carefully. Cut diagonally across the corners, crease up and stick the excess paper to the sides.

4 Cut a strip of paper to fit around the container, 1cm (⅜in) longer and wider than necessary to allow for the join and the turnings. Stick this strip to the sides, starting close to a corner where the join will be less noticeable. The bottom edge should be flush with the base.

5 Trim away a small V-shape from the excess at each corner, so that the top edges can be turned without wrinkling or tearing the paper.
   Apply a little more adhesive if necessary and press down the turnings.

LAMPSHADES

THESE LAMPSHADES look very pretty but they should not be made too narrow as the heat generated by the light bulb can cause the paper shade to scorch and, in extreme cases, to burn. Both shades are made using purchased lampshade frames, available from craft shops and some department stores. If it is not possible to find a lampshade frame, it is quite feasible to use an inexpensive lampshade of a suitable shape, as has been done for the pleated lampshade project. Lampshades can be trimmed with purchased braid, carefully selected so that it does not overpower the decorated paper, or paper can be plaited to create a matching braid, which can then be glued in place.

~

MATERIALS AND EQUIPMENT

Basic equipment ● *purchased lampshade frames* ● *base paper* ● *very lightweight top paper* ● *thinned PVA or fusible webbing* ● *pressed flowers or paper pieces* ● *iron* ● *impact adhesive* ● *needle and thread* ● *Japanese paper or lens tissue or modelspan paper* ● *dyes* ● *lightweight paper* ● *pair of compasses or string and pencil* ● *bone folder or smooth pointed wooden stick* ● *self-adhesive film*
. . . . . .

The simple round shade has been made with laminated paper (see page 23). Measure the circumference of the lampshade and cut a piece of the base paper, which is 3cm (1in) longer than this measurement and 1cm (⅜in) wider than the height of the lampshade. The shade will curl around the frame more easily if the grain runs from the top to the bottom. If the shade is wider at the bottom than the top, the piece of paper will form a slight curve and should be planned on a piece of scrap paper. Prepare the base paper as described in the section on laminated papers (see page 23). Lay the pieces chosen for the design in place and attach the top paper. The whole sheet can be covered with clear self-adhesive film to give the shade a wipeable surface.

1 On the wrong side of the paper, draw a faint pencil line slightly less than 0.5cm (½in) from the top edge. Draw another line below this, which is the thickness of the metal wire of the frame away from the top line.

2 Pierce holes on both lines through the paper, approximately every 4–5cm (1½–2in). The holes should be above each other.

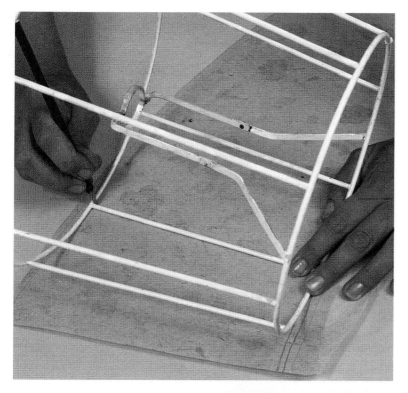

3 Lay the frame on the paper and
mark the position for the
bottom line, so that the previous
two steps can be carried out at the
lower edge. Trim the paper if
necessary.

Apply adhesive to the edges of
the paper that will overlap the
top surface of one edge and the
under surface of the other edge.

4 Position the paper carefully
around the lampshade frame.
It is often helpful to attach small
pieces of masking tape to the upper
and lower edges to help keep the
shade in the right place
temporarily. Alternatively, borrow
a second pair of hands.

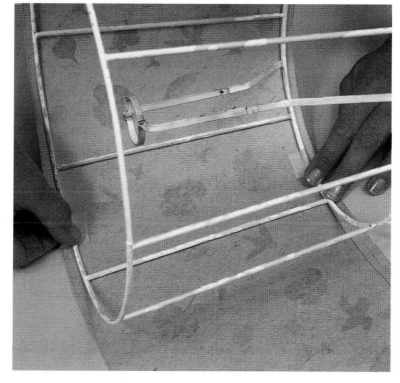

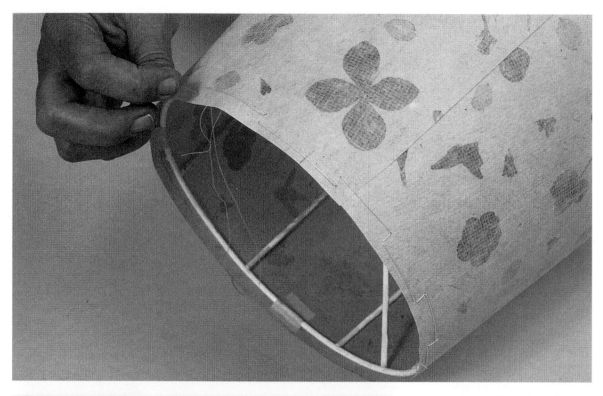

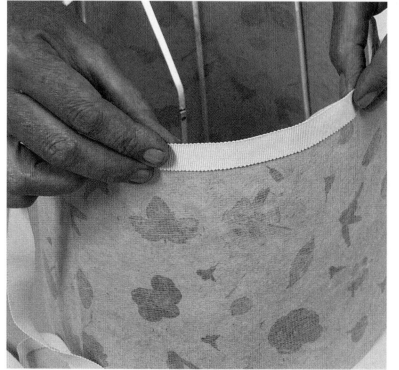

5 Thread a needle with toning thread and, sewing through the holes, fix the paper shade to the frame. From the inside, pass the needle to the outside and back through the corresponding hole below the wire frame and tie securely. Now repeat this step and then move on to the next set of holes. Without pulling too hard, pass the needle out and in twice so that the thread goes around the frame.

Repeat this process at the other edge of the lampshade. This completes the project.

6 However, the lampshade can be trimmed with a braid, which would cover the stitching and give a more finished look.

LAMPSHADES

The pleated lampshade is much more time-consuming to make but looks so lovely when it is finished that the time and effort are worthwhile.

This example has been made from folded and dyed paper (see page 22). You will need a lot of paper which you should prepare in the course of one session so that there are no colour variations.

The shade is made by pleating semi-circles of paper. The wider and flatter the shade, the more semi-circles will be required. If the shade has steeper sides, less paper will be needed.

Measure the height of the frame and add a third to this measurement, which will become the radius for the semi-circle. Three or four pieces of this size will be needed for one shade, unless the shade is for a wall bracket, in which case one semi-circle will be enough.

When you have decorated the paper, mount it on to a base paper: choose a lightweight paper so that it will pleat easily and neatly.

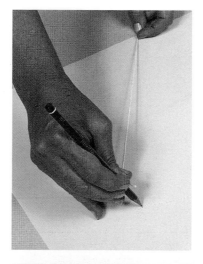

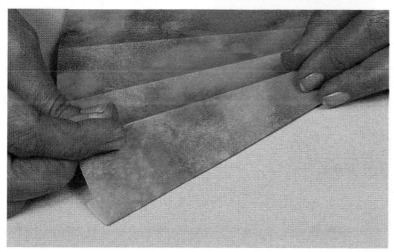

1 Draw semi-circles on the wrong side of the sheets of paper. If the radius is larger than the range of a pair of compasses, tie a piece of string to a pencil, fix the string in the middle of the top edge of the paper and, holding the string taut, draw an arc. Mark the central point before removing the string, as this will be used when pleating.

2 Cut out the semi-circles and make marks on the wrong side every 4 or 5cm (1½ or 2in) along the curve. With a ruler and bone folder, score from each mark to the central point and crease.

3 Now turn the paper over, right side facing, and carefully place the lower edge of one fold against the next one and pinch together, thereby marking the position for the reverse fold, which will create the pleat. Repeat this process all the way around the curve.

4 Starting with the paper flat and with the right side up, carefully fold and crease the reverse pleat, using the existing folds to help keep the pleats even. Work towards the middle from each side – it may make it easier to fold if a slit is cut at the central point.

5 When all the semi-circles have been pleated, trim them to fit. Cut the bottom edge straight first while holding the folds firmly in place. Measuring from this edge, cut off the tops of the pleats so that the piece is a little longer than the height of the frame.

6 Make a mark on the folded strip about 5cm (2in) from the bottom edge and, with a needle, pierce a hole through all the layers in the middle of the fold.

7 Glue the pleated strips together so that they form a continuous piece. Thread a needle with thread and pass it through the holes, starting and ending on the wrong side. With the frame propped up, either on the lamp or a box, position the shade on the frame and pull up the thread so that the pleats are held and the shade does not slip down. Tie the thread and trim the ends.

PICTURE MOUNT

IT IS POSSIBLE to use a stencil to decorate a mount
for a picture or photograph without going to a great
deal of trouble. There are suitable stencils available
ready-made or you can design your own. If the mount
is for a specific picture or photograph, an element from
the picture can be used to create the stencil; alternatively
a more traditional approach, which suits general needs,
can be chosen. The mount can either be purchased, or
cut to fit if the picture is an unusual size.

~

**MATERIALS
AND EQUIPMENT**

● *Basic equipment* ●
*purchased mount or mount
board and mount cutter* ●
stencil material ● *coloured
pencils* ● *scrap paper* ●
masking tape ·

· · · · · ·

TIP
Prepare the mount to the chosen
size or take a purchased mount
and, on a piece of scrap paper,
draw around the outside and the
window, being careful not to make
any marks on the mount.

1 Take the prepared stencil and,
on the scrap paper, draw the
shapes to ascertain whether the
planned design looks pleasing and
well balanced. The example shown
here has been carried out using
coloured pencils, which give a soft
appearance.

2 When the design is right, the
stencil can be fixed in place on
the mount with small pieces of
masking tape, which can be easily
removed without marking. Work
the design methodically and when
the first area has been finished, lift
the stencil and reposition it to
complete the design.

3 If you are using paints and
commercial stencils, the stencil
will have to be removed and the
paint allowed to dry before more
colours are added so that no
smudging occurs. These stencils
usually have dotted lines printed on
the second area to be coloured that
act as registration marks.

PICTURE FRAME

THIS PROJECT offers almost unlimited possibilities and uses easily mastered techniques. The biggest problem will be in deciding which type of decorated paper to use as so many of them will look effective. Marbled and paste papers, which generally have an overall design, are suitable as are stencilled or block-printed papers, which have been especially designed for the frame. It is important to remember the grain direction of the paper when making this project.

~

MATERIALS AND EQUIPMENT

● *Basic equipment* ● *thick card for frame* ● *marbled paper for covering* ● *plain toning paper for lining* ● *thin card for spacers* ● *PVA adhesive* ● *brush for adhesive* ● *scrap paper* ● *bone folder*

· · · · · ·

1 Cut two pieces of thick card to the required size and cut a window in one of them for the frame front. It is worth considering the size of standard photographs and enlargements when deciding the dimensions of the window, but do not make the window border too narrow as it will look rather unattractive.

2 Cut a piece of the plain toning paper, which is the same width as the frame and 2cm (¾in) longer. Stick this to one side of the frame back, neatly turning the excess piece over to the other side.

3 Cut the spacers about 1.5cm (½in) wide, two the same length as the frame, and one to fit between the two sides and across the top of the frame. Stick these in position and set the frame back to one side.

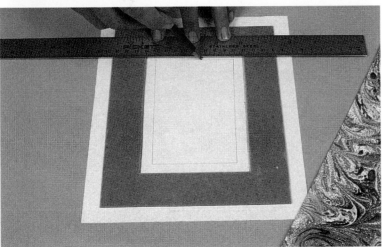

4 Take the frame front and cut a piece of marbled paper, which is 3cm (1¼in) wider and longer than the frame front. Lay the frame in the middle of the piece of paper and lightly draw around the window. Remove the frame and draw another line 1cm (⅜in) away, towards the middle. Cut out this smaller window.

5 Apply adhesive to the frame front and, using the pencil line as a guide, position the frame front on the paper. Check that there are no wrinkles, cover with scrap paper and smooth over with the bone folder. Cut into the corners of the window with the craft-knife, apply adhesive to the turnings and neatly stick to the wrong side.

6 Cut diagonally across the corners of the marbled paper, allowing for the thickness of both pieces of the card. Apply adhesive to the turning allowance at the bottom edge only and stick down neatly. Apply adhesive to the spacers and stick the back to the front.

7 Next, apply adhesive to the remaining turnings and stick them neatly in place, thus hiding the join on three sides; the picture or photograph will be slipped into place through the fourth side.

Cut another piece of marbled paper, which is 1cm (⅜in) less in length and width than the overall size of the frame. Stick this in position in the middle of the frame back.

Cut a piece of card for the strut. The length and width will depend on the size of the frame, but as a guideline the strut should reach the middle of the frame when glued in position.

Cut a piece of marbled paper, which is 1cm (⅜in) larger at the sides and pointed end of the strut, and 3cm (1¼in) longer at the top. Apply adhesive to the paper and stick the strut in place, turning in the sides and pointed end, but leaving the 3cm (1¼in) extension free.

Picture FRAME

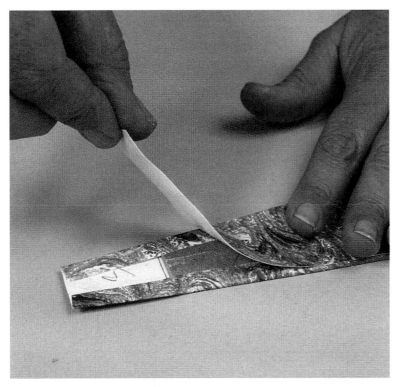

8 Cut another piece of marbled paper, which will cover the other side of the strut. This will be the wrong side of the strut and the extension should be bent in this direction.

9 Cut a small piece of marbled paper 3 x 6cm (1¼ x 2¼in) to make a strut strap. Fold and glue this piece so that a strip measuring 1 x 6cm (⅜ x 2¼in) is obtained. Fold this in half and crease both ends a little so that adhesive can be applied.

Stick the strut strap about 5cm (2in) from the strut point. Then apply adhesive to the other end of the strap and to the strut extension and place in position on the frame back, with the corner a fraction in from the frame corner.

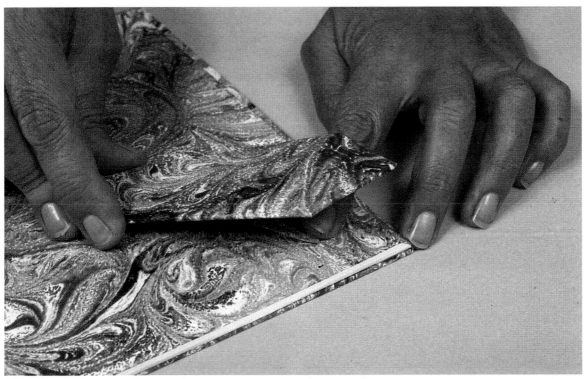

BLOTTER AND LETTER HOLDER

THE BLOTTER AND LETTER HOLDER shown in this project are only two of the items which can be made as desk accessories. Using the techniques shown in the various parts of this book, a sizeable matching set could be built up – including wastepaper basket, tub for paper-covered pencils, photograph frame, covered loose-leaf file, notepaper holder and stamp tray. It is advisable to give the project some thought so that you design the papers for economical use – it would be extremely frustrating to run out of matching paper in the middle. When selecting papers for the various items in the set, consider the balance of the overall look and do not be afraid to use plain toning paper as part of the design, as in the blotter corners, and not only for unseen linings, as in the letter holder.

~

MATERIALS AND EQUIPMENT

● *Basic equipment* ● *thick card for blotter and letter holder* ● *thin card for blotter corners* ● *cotton fabric for reinforcing letter holder* ● *marbled paper* ● *plain toning paper* ● *blotting paper* ● *PVA adhesive* ● *brush for adhesive* ● *scrap paper* ● *bone folder* ● *impact adhesive for assembling letter holder* ● *masking tape*

. . . . . .

THE BLOTTER

1 Cut a large piece of card. The size of the blotter is limited only by the size of the sheets of paper being used for the project. However, a good size for a blotter is 42 x 30cm (16½ x 12in).

First cover one side of the card with paper, using the technique shown on page 32. It is entirely a matter of personal preference whether the paper is decorated or not. When trimming the corners, cut off an excessive amount to reduce the bulk in the corners and thus allow for the blotting paper to slip in easily.

2 Prepare the decorative corners. Decide on the size of the triangular piece to be used – this one has sides of 10cm (4in) and a diagonal of 14cm (5½in). Cut four pieces of thin card to these dimensions and ensure that the grain runs in the same direction on each piece used in the project.

Cover these reinforcing pieces with plain toning paper, allowing a 1.5cm (½in) turning along the diagonal side. Turn this over and stick down. Trim the other two sides flush.

3 When making the decorative overlay, it is best to make a template from thin card. Mark the covered reinforcement triangle on the template and include the turnings at the outer edges.

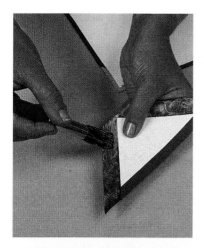

4 Cut four pieces of decorated paper from this template and, making sure that the paper is in the right position, stick one to each of the corners.

5 With the wrong side facing, score and crease along the card edges of each corner. Then mitre the corners, allowing for the thickness of the covered base.

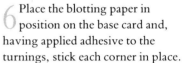

6 Place the blotting paper in position on the base card and, having applied adhesive to the turnings, stick each corner in place.

7 Finally, turn the blotter to the wrong side and glue a piece of paper, which is 1cm (⅜in) smaller than the blotter, to cover all the turnings. As before, it is entirely a matter of personal preference whether the paper is decorated or plain.

THE LETTER HOLDER

1 The letter holder is made from three pieces of card. Each piece is 20cm (8in) long. The back is 10cm (4in) high, the front is 8cm (3in) high and the base 6cm (2½in) wide.

The back and the front are stuck to the edges of the base, using the method explained in the Basic Techniques section. Spare strips of card 6cm (2½in) wide can be inserted towards the top of the front and the whole can be held in position with masking tape while drying.

2 Then cut a strip of cotton fabric a fraction less than 20 x 9cm (8 x 3½in) and stick this around the base with PVA adhesive to reinforce the joins.

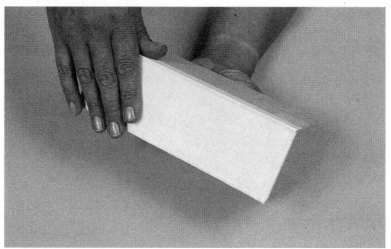

3 Cut a piece of decorated paper to cover the outside of the letter holder; the grain should run the same way as the card.

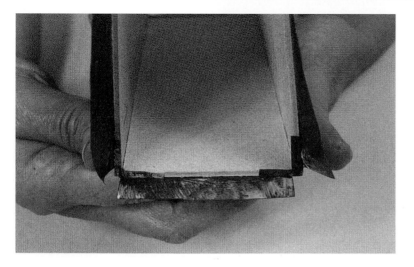

4 Referring to the Basic Techniques section on covering three-dimensional objects, carefully cover the letter holder, and mitre the corners neatly.

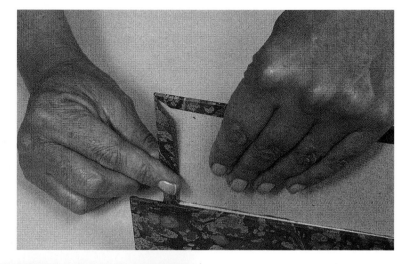

5 Next cover the inside of the letter holder with plain toning paper. Use a strip of scrap paper to measure the length needed; the width will be 1cm (⅜in) less than the letter holder.

6 This is a tricky operation as there is little space for manoeuvre but the correct grain direction will help, as the paper should roll down the back, along the base and up the front. Remember that the paper may stretch when the adhesive is applied, so do not be tempted to cut the paper too large. Choose a good quality paper that will not curl very much.

LETTER PORTFOLIO

THIS STYLISH PROJECT would make a wonderful gift. The portfolio can be adapted to different sizes but the one shown here is suitable for A4 papers. As with many of the projects in the book, the choice of papers is unlimited. The most traditional finish would be obtained if you use a marbled paper; in this example, more unusual paste papers have been used. If the portfolio is being planned as an art folder for a student, a block print designed by the student might be very appropriate. The spine and corners have been made from bookcloth, which is extremely durable, but it is only available at specialist shops. As an alternative, cotton fabric can be mounted on to paper, using the technique described for mounting paper on card in the Basic Techniques section. When the portfolio is opened the papers are revealed; the papers are kept in place by folded flaps on the three open sides of the holder.

~

MATERIALS AND EQUIPMENT

● *Basic equipment* ● *thick card* ● *paste paper for covering* ● *toning paper for lining* ● *bookcloth for spine and corners* ● *PVA adhesive* ● *brush for adhesive* ● *scrap paper* ● *bone folder* ● *chisel and hammer* ● *ribbon for ties*

· · · · · ·

TIP
The grain direction must run the same way for the card and the paper. A clean and well-organized work area will certainly help with the execution of this project as there are many stages. The adhesive should be kept out of the way until it is required and all waste paper should be removed from the work area, so that the adhesive is not accidentally transferred to it.

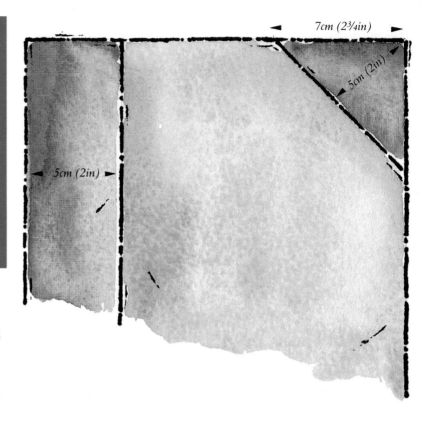

7cm (2¾in)

5cm (2in)

5cm (2in)

5cm (2in)

PREPARATION
Cut two pieces of board 34 x 25cm (13½ x 10in), preferably with the grain running the length of the boards, making sure that the corners are square. Draw a line down one side of each board, 5cm (2in) from the edge to delimit the edge of the spine cloth. Spine widths do vary but one fifth of the overall size of the portfolio looks about right.

Now draw a line diagonally across the top and bottom of each of the corners furthest from the spine marking – these should be 7cm (2¾in) from the corner points. The measurement from the corner will be the same width as the spine.

Decide how far apart the boards should be – the further apart they are, the more papers the portfolio will accommodate. In this example the boards are 2cm (¾in) apart. Now cut the bookcloth so that it fits across the two boards and the gap, allowing 1.5cm (½in) for turnings at the top and bottom – ie a strip 12 x 37cm (4¾ x 14½in). A second strip of bookcloth to line the inside of the portfolio spine is needed – this should be the width of the gap plus turning allowances of 1.5cm (½in) at each side and 1cm (⅜in) shorter than the boards ie 5 x 33cm (2 x 13in).

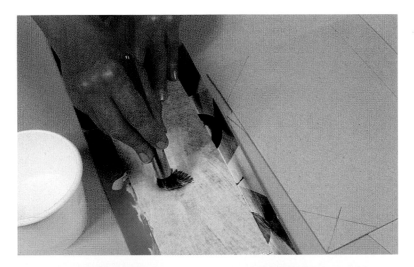

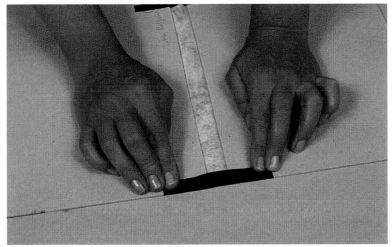

1 Lay the larger strip of bookcloth on a piece of scrap paper and brush PVA adhesive all over, working from the middle and making sure that all the edges are covered. Scrap paper from magazines with a slightly shiny surface is easier to use than old newspapers as the absorbent nature of newsprint prevents the brush from running smoothly.

Pick up the bookcloth, remove the scrap paper and place the cloth on the boards, positioning it between the marked lines. Cover the work with a piece of clean paper and smooth out by hand or with a bone folder. This will remove any air bubbles that may have been trapped. The covering of scrap paper stops the cloth from becoming shiny with rubbing or marked by dirty fingers or tools.

2 When the right side is smoothed, turn the work over and, applying more adhesive if necessary, stick down the turnings. Make sure that the bookcloth is pressed firmly into the space between the boards.

3 Now lay the smaller strip of bookcloth on a piece of scrap paper and brush PVA adhesive all over, working from the middle and making sure that all the edges are covered.

Pick up the bookcloth, remove the scrap paper and put the cloth on the boards, placing it on the wrong side for the spine lining. Cover the strip with a piece of clean paper and press into the space, working across from one side to the other while smoothing out any air bubbles.

4 Cut two pieces of bookcloth, which are 10cm (4in) square and cut across them diagonally. These will be used for the corners and an allowance for turnings has been made. Place the corner piece against the line on the board and, on the wrong side, mark the corner. Trim diagonally across the corner piece slightly outside the markings, so that a neat mitre can be made when the bookcloth is glued into position.

5 Brush glue over the corner piece and then position it against the line marked on the board. Turn over one side and, using the bone folder, neatly press the excess cloth against the board before turning in the second side. Repeat for the remaining corners.

6 Now take the decorated paper and select a suitable area from which to cut the two required pieces. These should be 37 x 21.5cm (14½ x 8½in) which allows for turnings and will let the piece of paper overlap the spine fractionally. Holding the paper firmly in position on the board, turn back the corners so that they overlap the cloth corners fractionally and crease them.

Take the paper away from the board and make a mark on the board and paper, so that they remain together as the two sides of the portfolio are unlikely to be identical. Trim off the folded area. Repeat for the other side.

7 Before glueing the papers in position, lay them in place on the boards and mark guidelines on the wrong side. Now, working quickly, so that the paper has as little chance to curl as possible, apply adhesive to it and carefully position on the board so that the spine and corners are just covered by the paper.

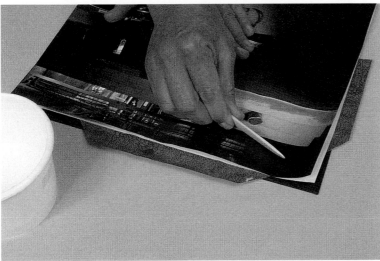

8 Cover the work with scrap paper and smooth, with the hand or bone folder, to remove any air bubbles. Turn the portfolio over and, applying more adhesive if necessary, stick down the turnings.

9 To make the ribbon ties, it is necessary to make a hole from the paper-covered outside of the portfolio to the inside. This is most easily done with a chisel but if a chisel if unavailable, a craft-knife or scalpel can also be used. First mark the positions for the holes – on both front and back boards – 1.5cm (½in) in from the opening edge and the width of the ribbon up from the middle. Using the chisel and a hammer on a piece of scrap board or wood, make the holes.

10 Cut two pieces of ribbon about 30–40cm (12–15in) long and push them through the holes. Position so that protruding bits can be glued towards the opening edge. Glue in place and then cover with the scrap board and hammer to close and flatten the incision.

The portfolio may now appear to have a slight curve – this is caused by the pull of the covering on the outside and will disappear when the portfolio has been lined. This is done in two stages: first the flaps are stuck in position and then the boards are covered with a single sheet of paper for each side.

11 Cut two strips of paper 33 x 10cm (13 x 4in), with the grain running the length of the strips, and four pieces 24 x 10cm (9½ x 4in), with the grain running down the short length of the pieces. Score a line with the bone folder 1.5cm (½in) in from the edge of each piece so that, when they are creased, the width will be 8.5cm (3½in). Neatly mitre the corners of the folded edge of the strips, which will meet, so that the layers of paper are kept to a minimum.

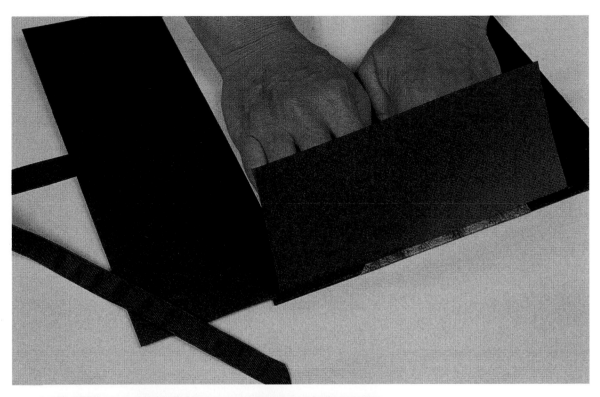

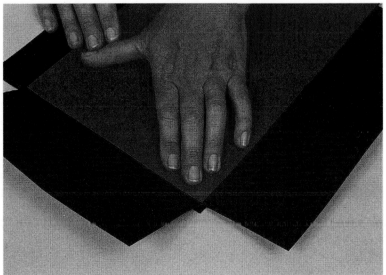

12 Apply adhesive to the folded turn-in of the long strips and stick in position 0.5cm (⅜in) in from the opening edge. Stick the remaining pieces in the same way at the top and bottom of each side of the portfolio, making sure that they meet the side flap at the opening edge.

13 Finally, cut a piece of paper for each side, 33 x 24cm (13 x 9½in). Check that this fits and neatly covers the flaps, which have just been glued inside, and trim if necessary. Carefully glue these pieces in place and smooth out with a covering of scrap paper so that all air bubbles are eliminated.

PHOTOGRAPH ALBUM COVER
AND PHOTOGRAPH ALBUM

Iᴛ ɪs ᴏғᴛᴇɴ difficult to find a photograph album with an attractive cover; if the album is being compiled to commemorate a special occasion, you can design an appropriate cover, perhaps by choosing the favourite colours of its future owner or by making a block print or stencil design that complements the subject of the photographs.

The photograph album itself can also be custom-made although it is a time-consuming project: the pages are cut to a size that suits the photographs, and the number of pages in the album is pre-determined by the number of photographs to be included in it. The colour and weight of the paper and card are also decisive factors in its finished appearance.

~

MATERIALS AND EQUIPMENT

● *Basic equipment* ● *thick card* ● *album sheets* ● *screwbinders* ● *decorated paper for covering* ● *toning paper for lining* ● *cotton fabric* ● *hole punch* ● *PVA adhesive* ● *brush for adhesive* ● *scrap paper* ● *bone folder*

· · · · ·

PHOTOGRAPH ALBUM COVER

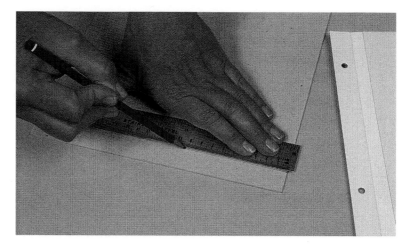

1 With the grain running from the top to the bottom, cut two pieces of card, which are a generous 0.5cm (¼in) wider and longer than the album sheets. Set aside one piece for the back cover.

Take the other piece and prepare the hinge, which will be needed to open the front cover. Measure the side strip of the album sheet, which has the holes punched, up to the middle of the flexible groove of the sheet. Mark this amount on the piece of card and cut off. From the remaining part of the card, cut off a further 0.5cm (¼in).

2 Now cut two strips of the cotton fabric 2cm (¾in) wide and the same length as the boards. These will be glued between the pieces cut in the previous step to act as a hinge – the paper on its own would be too vulnerable to being torn.

Lay the back cover board on the work surface and align the edges of the two pieces for the front cover on top. Apply adhesive to one cotton strip, place over the gap between the boards and press in place. Allow to dry for a few minutes, turn over and stick the second piece of fabric on the other side.

4 Next mark the position for the holes. Lay an album sheet on the back cover and, working through the holes in the sheet, mark the position of the holes on the covered board. Take the hole punch and, preferably working from the right side, make the holes.

3 Cut two pieces of decorated paper to cover the boards. These should have turnings allowances of 1.5cm (½in) on all sides. If the turning on the hinge piece is wider than the hinge piece, it should be trimmed to the same size. Cover the back cover as described in the Basic Techniques section.

Extra care should be taken when covering the hinged board for the front cover. Having applied the adhesive to the paper, place the paper on the larger board and lay it down towards the hinge part, pressing the paper firmly into the fabric groove. When sticking down the turnings on the wrong side, make sure that they are worked into the groove (see the Letter Portfolio project) but do remember that the paper is not as flexible as the bookcloth.

Now cut the toning paper for the lining. This should be about 0.5cm (¼in) smaller than the covered boards. Stick the lining for the back cover in place. Take extra care when sticking the lining to the hinged front cover to ensure that the paper is worked into the groove.

5 Place the two boards together using the back cover as a guide and, through the back cover, punch holes in the hinged section of the front cover.

6 Assemble the album. Unscrew the screwbinders and, from the outside, push the longer part through the holes in the back cover. Put the album sheets and the front cover on top and screw in the remaining part of the screwbinder. Alternatively, tie the album with ribbon passed through the holes.

MATERIALS AND EQUIPMENT

● Basic equipment ● thick card for covers ● paper or lightweight card for album sheets ● dividers, if available ● decorated paper for covering ● toning paper for lining ● bookcloth ● screwbinders ● hole punch ● PVA adhesive ● brush for adhesive ● scrap paper ● bone folder
. . . . . .

PHOTOGRAPH ALBUM
TIPS

As with so many projects, the first decision has to do with the size. For this project it will be necessary to cut the pages first and, therefore, the photographs should have been previously selected. The photographs for which this album has been designed commemorate a trip and can be displayed several to a page. Wedding photographs are best displayed one to a page.

PREPARATION

Add 2.5cm (1in) to the width of page you want – this will act as the hinge strip, through which the screwbinders will be fixed. The grain should run from top to bottom. Additional strips should be cut which are the width of the hinge piece and the length of the sheet. These will be placed between the pages, so that the album closes flat without bulging after the pictures have been stuck in place.

3 Now cut the covering materials. The bookcloth, or paper-lined fabric, will be used on part of the cover and the hinge. The decorated paper will be stuck to the remaining part of the cover. In this example, the bookcloth accounts for one fifth of the width of the cover. It will also be necessary to cut an additional piece of bookcloth to line the hinge and groove and, finally, toning paper to line the inside.

1 When the pages and strips have been cut, the pages should be scored so that they will turn easily. Using the dividers, set them to the width of the strip and mark this distance at the top and bottom of each page at one side. Lay the ruler against the two marks and score this line with the bone folder.

2 The holes can now be made in the hinge area of the pages. Decide on the number of holes: if the album is more than 20cm (8in) in length, it is probably best to have three holes. Mark their position in the middle of the hinge area about 5cm (2in) from the top and the bottom of the page. A third hole should be centred between the other two. Make matching holes in the interleaving strips. Now set aside the pages and prepare the cover.

Remembering that the grain should run from top to bottom, cut two pieces of thick card 1cm (⅜in) greater in length and width than the pages. Cut two strips of card the same length as the covers and the same width as the hinge area. If possible this card should be thinner than the covers.

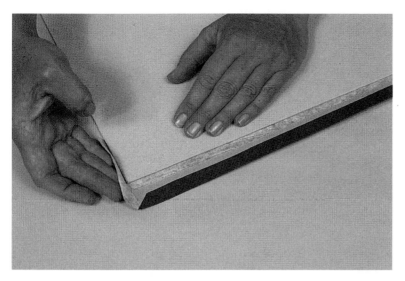

4 Prepare all the pieces and apply adhesive to the larger piece of bookcloth. Stick it in place on the front cover.

Then place the hinge piece on the bookcloth, leaving sufficient space of about 0.5cm (¼in), for the board to turn right over. Mitre the corners of the hinge and turn in the other edges.

5 Apply adhesive to the lining strip and stick in place. Next stick the decorated paper to the rest of the cover, turning in the edges neatly (see Basic Techniques).

Then turn the cover over and stick the toning paper in place. Complete the other cover in the same way.

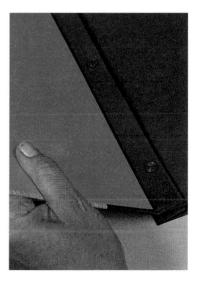

6 Mark the position of the holes on the hinge area of the cover using one of the interleaving strips as a template. Punch the holes as cleanly as possible.

7 With the right sides of the covers facing each other and the hinge pieces lying flat, place the album pages, with interleaved strips, between the covers and align all the holes.

8 Put the screwbinders in place and close the covers.

INDEX

Adhesive, 29

Basic techniques, 30–34
Block-printed papers, 18, 19
Blotter, 78, 79
Box cover, 52, 53
Box-making, 30–32

Covering with paper, 32–34

Decorating techniques,
    block-printed papers, 18, 19
    folded and dyed papers, 22, 23
    laminated papers, 23
    marbled papers, 24–27
    paste papers, 16, 17
    stencilled papers, 20, 21

Flanders, Dalma, 15
Folded and dyed papers, 22, 23

Gallery, 9–15
Gift bag, 48, 49
Glossary, 35
Greenburgh, Frances, 11
Greetings cards, 40, 41

Jones, Owen, 10

Laminated papers, 23
Lampshades, 60–65
Letter holder, 80, 81
Letter portfolio, 84–89

Marbled papers, 24–27
Materials, 28, 29
Measuring and cutting, 30
Mounting paper, 34

Notelets case, 44, 45

Papers, 28
Paste papers, 16, 17
Perry, John, 10
Photograph album, 94, 95
Photograph album cover, 92, 93
Picture frame, 72–75
Picture mount, 68, 69

Registration, 21

Scoring, 30
Sponging, 21
Spraying, 21
Stencilled papers, 20, 21

Von Clemm, Lisa, 12

Wastepaper container, 56, 57
Writing paper, 38, 39

ACKNOWLEDGEMENTS TO SUPPLIERS

The author and publishers would like to thank the following companies for their generosity in supplying the materials used to create the papers and projects in the book.

CHARISMA FRAMING

57, Station Road, Harrow HA1 2TY. Framers and suppliers of artists' materials.

T. N. LAWRENCE & SON

119, Clerkenwell Road, London EC1R 5BY. Suppliers of print-making tools and materials, and stockists of a wide range of papers, including specialist papers.

REEVES DRYAD

P. O. Box 38, Leicester LE1 9BU. Suppliers of artists' materials.

STENCILITIS

of Rickmansworth for permission to photograph some stencils from their range.

VILENE RETAIL

P. O. Box 3, Greetland, Halifax HX4 8NJ. Suppliers of interfacing and sew-in aids, including Bondaweb.

WIGGINS TEAPE AT PAPERPOINT

130, Long Acre, London WC2E 9AL. Suppliers of a wide range of machine-made paper and card.

WINSOR AND NEWTON

Whitefriars Avenue, Harrow HA3 5RH. Suppliers of paints and brushes.

The materials recommended are quite basic, and readers in Great Britain, Australia, New Zealand, South Africa and other parts of the world will have no problem in purchasing them at, or ordering them from, their local high street art and craft shops. Readers in North America can purchase by mail from: Daniel Smith Inc., 4130 First Avenue South, Seattle, Washington 98134, or from any good craft store or art and graphic supplies retailer.